4L

THE CLASS NEVER TAUGHT IN LAW SCHOOL

Greg R. Cohen, Esq.

CONTENTS

INTRODUCTION

Everyone knows lawyers, but very few like, or, more importantly, *trust* them. Lawyers make money off the misery of others. Car accidents, divorces, lawsuits, medical mistakes, harassment—it makes them smile. All they see is cash, cash, cash. And then there are a lot of cheesy commercials, inflated egos, and people who act like tough guys. What's there to like?

The fact is, for too many lawyers, the reputation fits: they are just a bunch of self-centered, arrogant, elitist know-it-alls. Do *not* become that type of lawyer.

But there are others out there who try to do the best for their *clients,* their referral networks, and other people. It is the right thing to do. The best part of this approach is that it's not only personally rewarding but it can be hugely profitable.

Why, then, would an attorney choose being a self-centered, arrogant, elitist know-it-all instead of someone who, quite simply, is a good person just trying to do the right thing for other people? It's simple: they don't get it, don't understand what their purpose is, and cannot see the big picture. They were never led down the right path because all they focus on are some "analysis techniques" they were taught in law school, or a tip or two from a peer to be obnoxious, mean, and tough so that everyone fears them. (In other words, they are know-it-alls being led by know-it-alls.)

This book, however, will take a different approach. It will help you understand that practicing law is not simply analyzing; it is about helping others, as well as developing and maintaining relationships. It is about the client who needs you, for which you should be thankful, not the client who should be thankful to have you as his or her attorney. The relationship between an attorney and his or her client should be treated no differently from those of family: there should be a bond.

This book will also teach you how *to give* business, which will lead you *to get* business—a tremendous amount of business. This is not a networking book. This is a book on how to give, live, and act, and with that comes business. In fact, if you are reading this on a shelf of a bookstore—granted one still exists—then turn to any page in Section III and read three lines. That's all it takes to receive a tip on how to create money for yourself.

That said, reading a couple of pages is not all you need. You need to change your philosophy for your entire practice to truly benefit. The best part, though, is that it's fun, it's rewarding to help people, and everyone, especially your clients, will get something out of it. What you will learn in the coming pages is real stuff from a *practicing attorney*. No marketing-analysis speculation here, just real business generation techniques. For twenty plus years, this is all I have done.

This book will cover all aspects of not only how to practice law but how to be a strong lawyer, consultant, friend, and business partner. This book will also teach you how to generate business and how to build a practice, so that you are no longer dependent on other lawyers to give you a share of *their* work, but rather, you will need other lawyers to do *your* work. This book will show you how to make serious money as a lawyer while still enjoying life, respecting yourself, and building a solid reputation. It is a guide for establishing sincere, long-term relationships that secure the bedrock of a successful law career.

As you will discover, I am not the greatest writer. In fact, I repeat myself a number of times. But this repetition exists for no other reason than that important points keep resurfacing. I continually want to remind you of those points, and I can only stress them so many times.

By way of introduction, I am a real estate attorney who has been practicing law for more than twenty years. I am board certified, which means the Florida Bar considers me an expert in real estate law. I have served as the chairperson of the Real Estate Section of the Palm Beach County Bar Association, and I give lectures to numerous groups, including lawyers for Continuing Legal Education (CLE) credits.

During law school, I was a B/B+ student. I studied a tremendous amount the first year, then slowed down a little to focus on the subjects I liked. Regardless, the grades were the same, I never missed a night out, and I was not going to be a "chosen one" for any law clerk or associate on "Legal Day."

After law school I went through a limited selection process and joined a midsize firm managed by my father. It was then that I realized that I did not know anything, except how to analyze an issue in the manner I was taught in law school. I did not know anything about practical issues, such as how to bill; how to ask for a retainer, certain federal and criminal laws, including those about bankruptcy and extortion; or even what purpose I was there to serve. I was a lawyer on paper, and that was all.

This book will jump-start every aspect of your practice so you will not be in the same position I was upon graduation. For experienced attorneys, it will enhance your ability to practice law immediately and help you further grow your business by using innovative ideas I have employed over the years. In fact, if even one new client comes out of the thoughts and ideas herein, you will already be benefitting.

I have broken the book into three and a half sections. (The half section, Section IV, is a final brief reminder so that you do not go to jail.)

The first section addresses the beginning of a career. It starts with understanding the interview process. Next, if you're fortunate enough to get employed, it will help you understand your value to your employer and your role.

The second section of this book focuses on how to practice law, whether it is your first day out of law school or if you are an experienced attorney. I want you to have an understanding of clients, the law, and how you can be a good attorney—or even a *great* attorney. For those of you already practicing, I want to help you bring yourself to a new level. It will teach you that being a lawyer is not simply raising your hand and shouting out the problem and answering, or just doing what I call "surface analysis." It is truly understanding the problem from every perspective, analyzing all the outside elements that affect the problem, knowing the players and the goals of the client, as well as how to treat a client and how to bill a client, among other lessons.

It's important to realize that the problem with your first day of work as a lawyer is that you basically have no clue. Hopefully your brain has been trained to analyze problems, but without practical application, you are essentially a puppet with a law degree. At that point, you also have very limited business skills to understand what it takes to survive as an attorney. Your first goal as an attorney is really simple: you need to become a good lawyer. This book—and in particular, Section II—will teach you exactly how to achieve that goal. For those of you who are forced to read this book in any prelaw collegiate class or any law school, or, even worse, by your parents, you will truly learn what it means to represent someone and be a real attorney. For experienced lawyers, this book is meant to remind you what is important when representing someone, as we were never taught this information but had to learn it on the job.

At this stage in my life, my clients and peers recognize me as an excellent attorney. I want you to have an idea of how you—even if you have always been a B/B+ student or were an average attorney for years—can attain such respect, and more importantly, *believe* that it is true. Many lawyers don't know these things after years of practicing and simply go with the flow and do a decent job. This book, however, will help you excel and reach an elevated level of practicing, and Section II will eventually become your everyday reading/reminder of what it means to really practice law at the highest level.

The third section of this book focuses on generating business. This, by the way, is your second goal as an attorney: to bring in business. Without clients, you have no practice. Thankfully, generating business is where I excel. My personal practice generates a large number of fees every year, more than most who bill hourly throughout the state of Florida. I am known as a master networker who brings in business for myself and others. When I started, I had no idea how to do it, and fortunately, it just came naturally to me.

I am here to help you obtain the same results. Everything that I can put on paper about generating business is in this book. If you pay attention, you will generate business, too, and your value will significantly increase. In fact, you may even become the most valuable person at your firm.

Finally, Section IV touches briefly on a few random things to remember from day one onward so that you do not go to jail. It is brief, but focuses on a few problematic areas that young lawyers need to be aware of.

My expectations are that after you read this book you will (1) be ready for day one of practicing; (2) have sufficient knowledge of every aspect of being a lawyer to those who are not simply clients but rather people with whom you have relationships; (3) understand how to be a business-generating machine; and (4) appreciate and enjoy the practice of law.

Please note that no change is immediate, but in time, your approach, style, and *value* will be strengthened if you follow any of the hundreds of suggestions in this book, which have proven to be true in my experience.

As a sidenote, some of you may not require a review of the initial parts of this book regarding interviewing and other matters, and while I do recommend you read it, if you are so inclined, try jumping to Section II so we can discuss how you can better practice law.

THE BEGINNING: GETTING THE JOB

It's time to figure out how to get the job, and then recognize your value. This section will discuss how to interview well so that you can find and obtain the right job. After that, we will discuss basic components of being an attorney at a firm so that you have a grounded perspective on your employment role.

Chapter One

The First Date: Interviewing for the Job

The interview is always the key to getting the job. If it was not, then the only people who would get jobs would be the people in the front row of your class who ask all the questions to let everyone know how brilliant they are.

I love interviews. In fact, I enjoy not only giving them but getting interviewed. It is incredible how much you can learn about someone during an interview. The problem with interviewing when you're the applicant is that most people do not understand what the employer is looking to learn from the meeting, so they walk into an interview and it feels like an ambush. Hopefully this section will help you better prepare for any interview down the road, especially if I am the one sitting across the table from you.

PREPARATION

My first question to every applicant is, do you know anything about our firm? If you have not taken the time to read about our firm, it's an immediate strike three. You are *out*. Leave. All it takes is fifteen to thirty minutes to go online to read about the company you want to hire you. If I am going to take twenty to forty minutes out of my day to consider giving someone a job, I would hope they would have the courtesy of preparing for our encounter. The point is, be prepared to answer this question *every single time*.

Next, as part of your preparation, try to learn about the person interviewing you. Truthfully, I couldn't care less if a potential candidate knows anything about me (as long as they know the firm), but why not try to get to know the person conducting the interview? Who knows? Maybe you went to the same high school, college, or law school. It's impressive when a candidate brings up relevant information or tells me about a connection we share without me asking!

I once interviewed a candidate who reminded me of something we had in common that was listed on our firm's website: we were born in the same city. All of a sudden, this guy stood out because he had brought it to my attention rather than me baiting it out of him, or it never being recognized at all.

Lastly, before you embark on any interviews, *understand yourself*. Know your strengths and weaknesses, and figure out what makes you unique and an asset to the firm. If your grades are not so good, as mine weren't, talk about activities you participate in and other attributes you have, such as work ethic and focus. If everyone was hired based on a resumé and GPA alone, there would be no reason for an interview in the first place. (See the first paragraph.)

CONNECTION

The goal of every interview—on both sides of the table—is to connect with the other person. Do not forget that the person giving the interview also *wants* to connect with you in some way and consider you as a person, not simply as an applicant. Furthermore, they may see you as a younger version of themselves, which always excites the diligent interviewer. Always try to connect. All the nonsense that books about interviewing teaches you, simply comes down to what type of connection you can make with the person across the table, so you can be remembered. You like college football and it comes up that your interviewer does, too; you have connected. Once you have *connected,* you will be *remembered.*

Additionally, check out Facebook or LinkedIn for other information about the firm or person interviewing you. To be clear, I do not want to be stalked by someone, but if I went to the Steamboat Ski Resort and you saw pictures posted on my page, bringing up the fact that you like skiing could easily evolve into a personal interview or conversation that forges a connection so you are, once again, *remembered.*

FUTURE DEVELOPMENT

The next thing to remember is that an employer wants to hire someone with a strong work ethic and desire to learn . . . *the employer's way.* Everything I say to an associate during his or her tenure is valuable information, and any associate should want to grow as a lawyer, *my way.* An associate's goal is to learn the law in the same manner, and with the same approach, as the principal. When I meet someone who wants to learn my way—and more importantly, someone I can train *willingly*—then I've found an assignment I want to undertake. Remember, the person who interviews you has all the answers—without question. You need to be the person who wants to know those answers, too.

TIPS

Now, let's go over some basic principles that, apparently, are not that obvious to everyone in my experience:

1. Dress for the interview. Women, try to look professional and put together; do not dress provocatively. Nobody wants to hire the sexy, smoking-hot associate who looks like she could go out to a nightclub after the interview. There isn't much more to say on women's attire because the adage is true: most women get it, while most guys are idiots.

Guys, wear a suit and tie. Not a jacket with slacks, *a suit and tie*. Here is another novel concept for some of you: button the shirt to the top and pull the tie up. You see, I have been wearing ties and jackets my whole life, and if you put on a tie but do not button the shirt to the top, not only does it not count but you look like a clown. So if you want to work at the circus, feel free to not button. And also, grab a big tie—you will do fine traveling with the elephants.

Reminder - get a long-sleeved button-down that is supposed to be worn with a tie. Any men's store employee can tell you what shirts are meant for ties, and shirts that require stays in the collar are a good place to start. I love the attempted "Nantucket look" with a plaid or boating shirt with a tie: it tells us instantly that you do not get it. I am not saying you need to be a fashion guru, but you have to look the part, because if you will not look the part for me, you will not look the part *for a client*. There's an episode of *Curb Your Enthusiasm* where a client fired his lawyer because of the way he was dressed, and frankly, it was right on point. If all else fails, go with a navy suit, white shirt, and blue tie. It's not that hard to match (even for those with taste like me), and you will look the part. If possible, wear black, *polished* shoes, as well.

Why is it so important to dress properly? Well, if you dress poorly, it is disrespectful to the firm, the job, and the interview. You want the job, so do everything you can to get it, starting with wearing appropriate attire. Put yourself in competition with—or ahead of—other applicants, and do not dress like you are going to the circus, or, worse, like you are *part of* the circus.

2. Be early. Here is another laugh, but it seems some people need to be reminded not to be late. Let's think for a moment about the people who are late to interviews. The first thing I would wonder is how they will report to work if they are hired. Will they be on time for meetings? What about for court sessions? Understand?

It's really simple: *Do not just be on time. Be early.*

Also, when you show up early, tell everyone you are there *early,* including the receptionist and the assistant who seats you. Understand that if I hear an appointment is at my office early, I get irritated, as there is now pressure on me to start the interview early. But when my assistant tells me that the applicant *knows* they are early, then the pressure is alleviated. Do not forget: the principal's schedule is a priority over job interviews.

3. Practice. Go on as many interviews as possible to learn the patterns and to get comfortable. Remember, however, to stay focused. While you may gain some experience by "interviewing well" on this crusade, you always need to have focus and fear. (By the way, I do not believe that you learn to interview well at any stage. I believe you need to learn to *express yourself* well, and that will lead to a good interview.)

4. Answer truthfully. For all questions, the correct answer is not what you think they *want* to hear, but the actual answer. Do not be phony. Be yourself. Do not try to be what you think somebody wants. This is actually part of the art of being a lawyer: saying something that supports your position, even though another person may not agree. At least you have principles, and it is good to have and display those principles during the interview process.

What about questions regarding past employment? Remember, all past experience provided some benefit to you, no matter what the job. Cut the bullshit on telling the interviewer how you learned good work habits and responsibilities—that is all nice, but tell me what you *really* learned. When I delivered pizza, I learned how long it took to cook a pizza and how a restaurant operates. *That* is interesting. Every job provides something unique, and if you impress some new information upon the person interviewing you, who knows, they may be extremely appreciative. And with that, there is often a reward.

What about when it comes to getting fired, arrests, and other negatives? Always be truthful, but always have a legitimate reason for why it was not *entirely* your fault. You still always accept responsibility and admit fault, but recognize that there were some other factors. (E.G. If you've been arrested you might think along these lines: *I did it. I was with some friends. I was young and stupid. I have learned from it, and I will never do it again. My parents grounded me.*)

5. Be ready for trick questions. Some employers also like to be assholes and ask you trick questions. (It makes them feel good to be empowered, or maybe they read too many books or paid for tests or courses about interviews.) For example, would you lie for the company? Stand your ground and maintain your ethics, and your answer will always be correct.

SUMMARY

Hopefully you have absorbed some of the above information to transform yourself into a true candidate for an interview, not just some intellectual parrot with no true substance and an unbuttoned shirt. Would anyone hire a person with straight As every year and the highest score on the bar if he or she showed up in shorts? Would they hire a phony? Would they hire a person without integrity? Not a chance.

Remember to strive for a connection, be honest and truthful, and always make sure your ethics trump everything else.

And don't forget, these things matter *all* the time.

Chapter Two

Meeting the Parents: Starting the Job

So you have the job. Congratulations. Now we need to go through some basic points of starting the job. Everyone should remind themselves of the points in this chapter when working for someone else.

You show up the first day, walk around, and meet everyone. Everyone is so nice to you and for those first forty-five minutes you love being a lawyer, without even having practiced law. Then you realize you know nothing.

The truth is, for the next fifty-two weeks of your life you will be completely lost. You passed the bar, but you have no clue what to do or how to be a lawyer. Before you pass out, be sure to remember *who, what, where, when, why,* and *how.* Every legal issue and question should be analyzed starting with those basic questions. Once you are done with that analysis, try the same analysis from the opposite side. At least you now have a little thought process to apply to your assignments. Back to work.

How do we start? I think we need to start with a problem that I see in modern society: young associates believe that they have status, and worse, are *entitled*. They feel special and value themselves to a degree well beyond their status. I am not sure where this new generation of millennials developed the idea that they do not have to work for a number of years before any entitlement will be provided to them. To address this growing belief of young law students, associates, et al., I thought I would give you some reminders, thoughts, and tips on how to be a better employee before I teach you how to practice.

UNDERSTANDING YOUR ROLE
(FROM THE PRINCIPAL'S POINT OF VIEW)

It's important to remember who you are and how you look to your employer. Here are some of the most commonly forgotten or ignored understandings:

1. You are not *that* smart. You may be a first-round draft pick, but you need to develop into a good attorney. In fact, many first-rounders do not work out, especially if they do not understand the big picture (about eight professional quarterbacks come to mind). I don't care that you have a 4.0, it does not mean that you will live up to your expectations. Do not think you are special. You are entitled to nothing. You are just a pledge.

From my perspective, a young practicing lawyer should be *thankful* for his or her job. Your employer has made a commitment to you for any number of reasons, and truthfully, to me, you are one of a million other people who have not accomplished much in life. If you think you are special because you graduated from a good college or law school like Harvard, Yale, or the "U", or because you booked a class (for those of you who do not know what this means, it means you received the highest grade in the class, but I never had any personal experience to validate), I would like to remind you that neither I nor anyone else cares. It is a personal accomplishment if you had the highest LSAT or bar exam score, but all it means in the real world is that you are smart or that you test well. A new associate, clerk, or intern needs more than that—a lot more than that. You need to have hunger and drive. You need to remember—and *feel*—that your goal is to earn the respect of your employer through diligence, dedication, and humility.

2. The principal's schedule and terms come first. I want an associate to meet me on my terms and schedule. You make yourself available when I am available. If I say Saturday, you meet me on Saturday. If I say 5:30 p.m., you meet me at 5:30 p.m. Your schedule is totally subject to mine. And do not forget, associates, that private meetings after business hours are also good times to ask questions. Principals do want you to have questions—even hypothetical, ridiculous questions—but they want you to have them on *their* time.

3. Deadlines are important. My biggest complaint about young workers is they do not understand the rules, and deadlines even less so. You need to understand that an assignment given to you on Friday at 3:00 p.m. that is turned in on Monday at 3:00 p.m. has taken *three* working days, not one working day. Saturdays and Sundays are *working days*, and e-mailing to let me know you worked on the weekend does not impress me. Weekends equal two working days.

4. Fit in. No matter what anyone says, an associate must have some brainpower, but most importantly, you *need* to fit in with the firm. See, if you are working at my firm, and I do not like you, you will either need to adapt to my practice or I will run you into the ground. If you happen to have a connection with me, then I will do everything I can to help you, just as you would rather help a friend than an enemy or someone who annoys you.

5. Be aware of the reality. If you do not like to hear how inferior you are, go pledge elsewhere because there are other people who are willing to commit to this work ethic and the rules above.

If you do not believe me, look at the successful principals of the major law firms in your area. Most of them possess certain powerful characteristics, even if some, like myself, did not have the greatest grades in law school. We all listened and obeyed in our early years.

6. You are not entitled. When does entitlement start? For the purposes of this book, the answer is *never*. In reality, it *will* develop, but it takes time—years and years. If you do not understand this, you will have problems in *every* employment relationship you experience. Entitlement only comes once you have followed the rules of the game above, have done as much as you can to better yourself, and have earned some respect.

As to discussing entitlement, you are permitted to ask what the plans are for you, if any, in the future. This does not mean

"Can I become a partner?" This means, as a clerk, "I am hopeful I can continue working here next summer and possibly after law school, if you will have me." This means "I am hopeful I have done what was asked and I would ask you for any ideas or suggestions on how I can improve." You are still a nothing, but a nothing with heart and dedication—if you are humble and recognize this—and your employer should see it, as well.

Many people in the younger generation believe they are entitled to perks on day one, which is the complete opposite of the view of older generations. Entitlement is something you earn. Be like the older generations and earn your entitlement. That is who I want in my firm.

Once you learn your role, you can earn a little respect and plant the memory that you are worth something because of what you are able to give. That will distinguish you from other attorneys, help you succeed at the early stages, and develop that coveted entitlement.

TIPS FOR SURVIVAL

Surviving in a law practice isn't as difficult as you might think. If you follow the below tips, you'll be much more prepared to succeed.

1. Find out who you report to and/or who oversees your work. This is the most important person in the firm. They can make you or break you. Do not kiss their ass or suck up, but do everything they ask as if it is the most important task in the world.

2. The lawyers who work the hardest are the ones who excel. You should be thankful for the opportunity to work, so you need to live and breathe the firm and its principals. If you have the work ethic and the education, job security and money will follow.

3. Listen to the goals that are set for you and always exceed them. If you are ten hours behind on a Saturday, wake up early. Do not be the person who misses the most basic concept of making money for the firm by failing to reach your goals.

4. Try to experiment with as many areas of law as you can and get as much experience in as many different fields as possible. You will not become an expert in an area in three years, but here is a tip—nobody can. Truthfully, different areas help you decide what you like best, and what you do best.

5. Volunteer. Always be the first one to volunteer and to attend any firm events or outings. Naturally, you would rather sit at home and do anything else, including reading a romance novel, but this is your way of saying the firm comes first. I have had many associates over the years who work hard but have never gone out of their way for the firm. All this means is they do not get it. If you want to be a partner and, more importantly, earn some respect, the firm comes first. (Coincidentally, I do not get mad anymore when young associates do not attend these events because I know I will be able to retain them at a lower salary for a long time because they do not get it.)

6. Try to establish an alliance with someone senior to you, who does not feel threatened by you (i.e. a person much higher on the ladder). This will be the person higher up the ladder than you to whom you can ask stupid questions and get helpful guidance. Although there are no stupid questions to some people, there are stupid questions to me, so do not waste the time of main superiors, but refer to a friend.

7. Every assignment is both a priority and a rush. Even if you treat something as unimportant because you think it is small, it still may be very important to the person who asks. Every assignment I have ever given out is important to me. Treat everything that way. I want someone who gets the work done well *and fast.* I want someone who works like I did when I was younger—if the firm was open over the weekend, Monday mornings are not meant for Friday assignments, they are for new emergencies. So if your principal is waiting for you to finish the Friday assignment on Monday, he or she won't be very happy. Your schedule is never set because every issue/emergency is passed on to you as the new associate. For an associate, the only predictable thing about your job is that your schedule is unpredictable, so do not wait until Monday to do something.

8. Follow up. Always let the person who gave you the assignment know where you are. This is a particularly good practice when someone asks you to make a phone call—an e-mail telling me that a call was made makes me happy, as I do not have to waste my time reminding you or asking if you followed through. Again, follow up. I mean it. Follow up.

SUMMARY

To make it, you must be a good worker, try not to get too caught up in yourself, and remember the basics, which will help keep you grounded and focused.

EXCEL AT THE PRACTICE: HOW TO BE A GREAT LAWYER

For those of you starting to practice for the first time, do you want to be average or great? Truthfully, even if you just want to be average, this section will assist you, because you have no clue what it means to be a lawyer.

For those of you who have been practicing, perhaps you understand some of the information set forth, as you had to learn it on the way. Regardless, this section encompasses everything I believe you need to know to rise above the rest in practicing law. It teaches you how to practice from every perspective, it makes you analyze each situation in a different manner than ever before, and last, it teaches you to understand the client.

If you follow *any* of the lessons herein, you will be a better attorney. If you follow most of them, you will be a great attorney.

Chapter One

What Needs to Be Done

This is where we really get rolling.

Now that you've been given some basic tips and have an understanding of how to deal with work ethic and meet certain goals, it is time to learn what distinguishes an average lawyer from an excellent one. Do not forget the aforementioned work ethic—people want winners who try to exceed goals, not the average who meets them. The prior section of this book has hopefully been a little helpful in teaching you how to start practicing (and get a job), but the real focus, and basically what you really need to know, is how you can become the best attorney around, whether you are fresh out of law school or an experienced attorney. The best practicing attorney is not only someone who advocates well, but someone who understands the client and the entire situation.

Let's look at what I feel helps me to be a great lawyer in my day-to-day practice of law. You need to read this information and advice and practice it full time. There is no compromise.

ANALYSIS

All we learned in law school was analysis, to spot the issue. But that simple process requires more than just addressing your present-day assignments.

This is your new approach until you die: on every assignment, and/or new issue or problem, you must ask the basic questions of who, what, where, when, why, and how while *keeping in mind who your client is*. This will help you understand the problem and your client's concerns, rather than rushing to judgment. You must analyze the argument on its face, answering *each* of these questions. Once you think every item through on behalf of your client, create a list of points. Everything is fresh on your mind so write your thoughts down on paper (or type if you are a computer person) with some of the issues you think which are good and bad. File it and keep it as a reminder for some later time. Most attorneys touch client issues on the surface, but do not get into the problem to really understand the matter at hand. This simple approach will help you make great strides.

However, you are not to stop there. You must then ask the same questions—who, what, where, when, why, and how—from the opposite perspective, or from the other side of the matter. (Also, write it down.) It is this analysis that helps a lawyer truly understand the argument, as it is not just about the position of your client—you must understand the perspective/analysis of the opposing side.

One weakness of many attorneys is that they are simply reactive. Their entire practices are about routine work, and it is only after the other side responds or raises an argument that they then can begin to address the matter. Taking the time to analyze *both sides* will better prepare you for the opposition's arguments, as you will be able to anticipate their thoughts and, more importantly, be proactive to address them before they ever get there. You always need to know what makes the client and the opposition tick.

Additionally, if you ever have a moment in front of a client against the other attorney when you immediately respond to their arguments or points, your client will be impressed because you have obviously thought it through. In essence, if you practice this ritual in advance for every client, you will always have an advantage over the average attorney and you will begin to develop into a superior attorney. Furthermore, once the problem is understood and analyzed in this manner, you will no longer be reactive, but proactive.

THE GOLDEN RULE OF PRACTICING LAW

The next recommendation, which I consider to be the Golden Rule of Practicing Law, is to take your client's matters *personally*. This is not always the best approach from a health standpoint, and you have to remember that the best decisions are not made when emotional, but it is so important to approach your clients and their issues in this manner. Not only does it make you a better lawyer but your clients will have more confidence in you.

I often hear people, including attorneys, say, "Do not take it personally" and "Let it go." What the hell are they talking about? If I am supposed to represent someone to the best of my abilities, why wouldn't I give them the best treatment? I know of no level of representation other than doing my best. Why wouldn't I treat their problems as I would my own problems or my family's problems?

Clients are people with problems and they contact lawyers for help. Why not treat them as well as you can? Why not take it personally? Have you ever had a problem and a friend brushed you off, or even worse, did not at least empathize with you? You became angry at them because you felt bad and you wanted them understand what you were going through. Clients are the same—they want you to advocate for them, but also truly understand and *feel* their issues.

People come to me for representation because they know I care about them and their issues. (I still cannot comprehend how a lawyer can represent someone and not take it personally.) Losing that drive detracts from everything, including how you approach things, how the other side views you, and, most importantly, how your client feels about you. Clients want 100 percent; this treatment gives them the 100 percent they need, including the emotional 100 percent. (You will still need the work to back it up, of course, but this creates a bond.)

I have had lackluster, unemotional associates who every so often tell me that they cannot stand some lawyer on the other side and that they want nothing more than to beat that lawyer. That is taking the matter personally. My only request of them is to not limit that personal reaction to those situations alone that pertain to them and their feelings; apply it to all dealings on behalf of a client. You do not need to get mad, just make it personal.

You will learn that once you take a client's matters personally, you actually get to know the client better. You will not just be an attorney representing them, but someone who "gets it" from their perspective and someone who is therefore more efficient.

The easiest and quickest way to get to this level is to pretend your client is your mother, father, wife, husband, or child, and to visualize the other side as someone you despise. (For me, there are so many on my list, it is not hard to do.) You will immediately learn to practice taking your client's matters personally. When you fight for them like they are family, you become a better attorney.

If the other side (whether the attorney or your opposition) recognizes that you are taking this personal approach, they will also recognize that their battle will be harder. Every time you take a matter personally, you are a better lawyer than someone who does not. You now have an advantage, and it is again more beneficial for your client.

It is important to remember that clients' issues are personal and important to them, so when you treat their issues with the same feeling, you become a better attorney.

BE PASSIONATE

Expanding on the Golden Rule, once you take a matter personally, hopefully you will become passionate about the cause. An attorney who approaches a client's issues with passion obtains better results.

When you feel anger or wrath or sadness with your client, you have improved your connection with them. You are now one of them—a person who recognizes, or at least expresses to the general public, that your client's issues, no matter how big or small, are the most important issues in the world to not only them, but you. This also makes you appreciate your client's goals and not take anything for granted. The more you appreciate your client's position, the more you understand the issues and arguments.

I understand that it is hard to develop passion if it does not come naturally (anyone will tell you I am an intense, passionate guy—sometimes I even hear the term *angry*), so it is up to you to learn how to evoke passion. I suggest you revert back to recognizing the honor of being selected for the job when a client hires you. You should also be honored that the client has the confidence in you to allow you to represent them, or, just as important, that your superior has enough confidence to allow you to handle someone who looks to them for guidance. Once you recognize the gravity of that situation, and recognize that your situation is more than just "some client hiring a lawyer," hopefully you will feel some passion in returning the favor to those who have entrusted you with their problems. It is your responsibility to reward them by practicing law to the greatest degree, which will develop with passion.

LEARN TO COMMUNICATE WITH YOUR CLIENTS

Is there anything more important than communication with a client, whether it be providing explanations or following up? The biggest complaints about attorneys involve follow-up or, at a minimum, communication skills. Clients leave attorneys when there is no or poor communication. Clients need to hear results, and they need to know you are on top of their cases. They also need to feel good and communication assists with this.

Below are some suggestions for better communication with your clients. If you follow my advice, you will become a better attorney who communicates efficiently and effectively with your clients. In return, I assure you that your clients will be happier with you and feel better about trusting you, which is an important part of the process. As I said, the biggest complaint about attorneys is a lack of communication, so keeping your communication skills strong will propel you to the next level.

1. Everything is important to them. Do not ignore it. Ever tell a story that you think is funny or interesting but the party listening does not share the same enthusiasm? You hear "had to be there" and you think, "What an inconsiderate _____ *(I will let you, the reader, fill this in.)* for not recognizing this meant something to me." You need to remember that everything a client tells you is important to them, so when you respond, you need to be very conscious of that. Do not downplay their

4L – THE CLASS NEVER TAUGHT IN LAW SCHOOL | 35

thoughts, even if those thoughts mean nothing in the context of a legal analysis or to you personally.

2. Always be upbeat. Clients do not like depressed attorneys (this will be discussed later, as well).

3. Always be personable. Clients want attorneys that are easy to speak with. Good people. Clients prefer good attorneys that they get along with.

4. Always make them the most important client. As far as they're concerned, they are your only client, and they want to know that you're pulling for them. Saying things like "You know I want this for you" is one way to help them feel like they matter to you.

5. Always be confident and tell them you are in control. You want to instill them with a sense of trust and confidence *in you*. Use the phrase "Here is what I am going to do" to show them that you have a plan that will work. When you go to a doctor, you want the doctor to tell you what to do, not dance around with a million hypotheticals.

6. Always let them in on some of the chess match. Let your client know that you have thought out the process. Share with them what the opposition may do and what they may say, and how you plan to respond. Show them that you are anticipating and being proactive.

7. Always apologize when you are late. If you are running behind getting to a meeting with them, show them that they are a priority to you by apologizing when you arrive and letting them know you were rushing to get to them. A busy lawyer always appears successful, but you still need to be considerate.

8. Always give them your cell phone number. This tells your client that you have a personal relationship with them. (Also, your cell phone number should be on your e-mail, so it should not be that much of a secret.) Some lawyers do not give out their cell phone numbers as they do not want to be "bothered" when their clients want to reach them. They only want communication on their terms, which is basically an ego problem for those attorneys. You will lose business and faith from a client as you are not accessible (see #9).

9. Always tell clients they can call you anytime. Again, an accessible attorney is one of a kind. The interesting thing is that the respectful clients only call if it is an emergency and most do not call on weekends because they do not want to bother you.

10. Tell them about your familiarity with the issues and your past experiences. However, avoid the *long* stories about your experiences and other clients. If you handled a similar matter, keep it brief, but let them know your history and experience. (If you are familiar with the topic, it should be easier.)

11. Always communicate your familiarity with the people involved in the case. Whether your knowledge relates to a judge, a bank, or something else, your client will feel more confident knowing you have personal relationships with the others involved in their case.

12. Give a client a deadline that can be met. You want to give people realistic expectations, so set goals that you can meet. If for some inexplicable reason a deadline cannot be met, give a new one, as well as a plausible excuse, such as having a new theory you are investigating.

13. Always e-mail a client with all your contact information immediately after meeting them. Additionally, thank them with a nice note after that first meeting and try to make the note as personal as you can.

14. Always act like you do not report to anyone. You are the be-all and end-all. As to principals, do not talk about or focus on how associates are doing work for you. Your fellow attorneys *assist* you. You are the boss.

This can be a difficult type of confidence to exude when you are younger, though, so any collaborative efforts should be characterized differently. For example, "We have weekly firm meetings when we all collaborate on every case to make sure everyone is thinking about what is best for you" sounds better than "I will check with my boss, Mr. Big Shot, and see what he decides."

15. Always tell clients why you are more expensive than the other guy . . . but only if they ask. Usually this comes down to experience, so make sure they know why you're the lawyer for the job.

16. Do not talk about yourself personally until they are done speaking about themselves and their issues. They are not there to learn about you until you have connected and expressed your desire and ability to help them.

17. Never act like you do not know the answer. This does not mean you guess, but there are mechanisms for responding when you do not know. Offer an educated guess on how it should be analyzed and assure your client that you will check it out, look into it, or get with an expert if it is not your area.

18. Try to keep clients in the loop with any news, especially good news. Always try to give them the good update rather than waiting for them to ask. The case is very important to your client, and you should get some credit if something good happens. I cannot believe how many times clients have called asking for updates on matters another attorney is working on, and there is actually good news that has not been relayed to the client. It is unacceptable to the law practice.

If you have to give someone bad news, try to be tactful about it. For example, you might say, "This is a problem, but this is how we are addressing it." Never let the client dwell on the loss or the problem if it can be won in the long run or is curable. Clients understand that issues and problems do come up, and they need to know you have solutions or ideas. Be prepared to list alternate approaches, and think them through before you call.

19. Follow up when there is no update because that *is* an update. Clients like knowing that you haven't forgotten about them and what is going on, even when there is nothing new to report. I would guess 10 percent of all attorneys take the initiative to follow up, and your clients will be bragging to others about how you reach out to them unsolicited.

20. Return phone calls. Not calling clients back is the quickest way to lose them. Clients need to communicate with you and the phone call must be returned within *one day*. No exceptions. If I can return sixty-five phone calls a day, then surely you can return twenty. Also, as an attorney, returning phone calls late at night is acceptable. You are thinking about the client after hours, and that is the kind of dedication they want to see.

21. Know when to call and when to use e-mail. If you follow the communication tips I've shared so far, you will be a better attorney who communicates well with his or her client. In return, I assure you that your clients will be happier with you and feel better about you, which is all part of the process. A great attorney is one who communicates with his or her clients efficiently and effectively. As I mentioned, the most frequent complaint made about attorneys is a lack of communication, so keep that communication so it propels you to the next level. But that's not all there is to it. One of the most common problems in communication today is deciding whether to call or e-mail. This is the danger zone for a number of attorneys.

When using e-mail, you are communicating, but you are not creating a connection with the client. You are hiding behind the computer and becoming a robot. E-mail is good sometimes, but not always. The main reasons most attorneys avoid direct communication and often hide from the clients are as follows:

A. They do not like them.
B. They have no good news.
C. They are not prepared.
D. They have no news and do not want to waste time.
E. They believe that e-mail is the same as personal contact.
F. They lack communication skills.
G. They do not understand that clients need personal contact.

I also believe this lack of communication is generational. The younger generations are so computer and tech savvy that they lose touch with the concept that actual direct telephone or in-person communication is necessary. Only sending e-mails and never speaking to clients will lead you to *lose* clients. (I appreciate the business you just sent my way because you could not pick up the phone. Thanks!)

As a general rule, you should never use e-mail when doing the following:

A. **Answering questions.** When it comes to confrontation or answers, some attorneys hide behind their computers rather than having direct discourse with their clients. Perhaps it buys them time with a difficult question, but that doesn't mean it's the right way to go. So let's start with this understanding: e-mail is the best for follow-up or checking in, but is the worst for responses that extend beyond ten words. You need to communicate those answers in person or by telephone with your clients.

B. **I remind you, e-mail *never* works if you are answering a hypothetical** with so many intangibles or if you are trying to solve a problem without specifics, as you cannot cover everything. Furthermore, e-mails in those situations are often misleading. There is always an intangible analysis (money, costs, etc.) for every problem, so solving problems requires a phone call, not an e-mail. I see legal malpractice matters that come in based on e-mail responses all the time. Lawyers who answer questions solely via e-mail often encounter events that could have been avoided if they had spoken to the client.

For example, a client sends you an e-mail asking if he can deed his house to his spouse. You say yes and that you can help with that. But instead, the client does the deed himself, and it turns out that the client's lender, with their prohibition against such transfer, is now foreclosing. The client then sues you, stating you did not disclose the problem points and he has the e-mail to prove it. Now you are stuck in a lawsuit because you sent an e-mail rather than calling the client and explaining the answer in full after asking all the correct questions.

Avoid the e-mail trap. Phone calls reveal many facts that are necessary for analysis, and should be employed when answering a legal question.

C. **Arguing.** What else does not work by e-mail? Arguing with someone. We all know the routine—the scathing e-mails between attorneys or, even worse, between an attorney and a client. Insulting and demeaning someone in an e-mail is not good for any reason. Why? Because it is in writing that can be saved and printed, and thus, it lasts *forever*. Just like incriminating pictures taken when you were young – they never go away. People will always remember and they will have proof of it. If you read an argumentative e-mail exchange after the fact, it also looks like two kids in a fight. Also, you capitalize words to yell at me? You are basically a joke.

When I receive an e-mail from a jerk, I make a point to forward the e-mail on to all attorneys in my office asking if anyone knows the sender. I also bring the e-mail to the next attorney meeting to discuss. The point is, I may have been a jerk to him or her, but all that will be remembered is the condescending e-mail that was written.

In summary, pick up the phone if you are going to fight and avoid the printout for the world to see.

D. Discussing billing. Discussions of billings with a client should always be conducted on the phone. It is harder for a client to argue on the phone than hiding behind a computer.

There are, however, times when e-mail is more appropriate:

A. When doing follow-up. The positive to e-mail is the quick follow-up, such as when you simply need to say, "I left him a message; no update yet." The client will see that you are working on the matter; if they fail to see that, they will go elsewhere. Clients do not like having to call for an update every two weeks. They believe you should provide updates unsolicited. Keeping them informed with brief updates saves you time and keeps them happy. Also, when waiting on a client, best to be proactive and reach out - "Have you received any updates regarding your insurance issue?"

B. When you are in a bad mood or feeling negative that day. Confidence is essential in practicing law to the fullest. Clients need it from you. If you are acting depressed, they will lose faith in you, or worse fire you. The client needs to trust you, respect you, and believe you are confident with your support of their case. They want someone who makes them feel good and comfortable. Using e-mail can help you keep whatever negative emotions you are feeling out of the interaction on that day.

22. Clients want positive communication. This also helps you control the client. If you are assertive, they will listen. If you are weak, it is more likely they will not listen. Other attorneys also get nervous if they see confidence. It promotes you in the best light, and you need to be confident to reach the next level.

Always emit confidence. In the last ten years, I have never walked into a closing room where I did not run the closing. This is confidence. My clients tell me there is a new air in the room when I walk in. Be confident and polite.

Every client wants to feel like they are going to win, so be positive when you talk with them. They want an attorney who is positive, strong, aggressive, and confident. Otherwise, they will not feel like you are their advocate, and you will lose control of the client, lose the edge created by such confidence, and, even worse, maybe even lose the client.

TALKING AND ACTING WITH CONFIDENCE

Building on the above, you need not only *be* confident but you need to talk and behave confidently.

I have a reputation of being an aggressive attorney. (Clients often use the term *bulldog* when referring to me.) Basically everything I hear draws an aggressive response from me, which always sends a positive message to the client, even if their case is not very strong. If you are aggressive, or at least speak with confidence, clients feel comfortable with you, which makes them more manageable and controllable. Understand that if you are nervous or weak, and you send that message to your client, they will sense it and you will instantly lose your ability to manage or control them.

And worse, they will start to second-guess everything you say.

For example, when I discuss any initial analysis, I remind the client of the "no guaranty" corny lawyer jargon. (I'm not sure who said it first, but apparently lawyers can *never* guarantee a win in a case.) I also remind them of the risks, but I focus on the *positive* aspects. Doing this creates a better environment in which to manage your clients, and they will feel better about you while also understanding the risks. You need to manage a client well in order to be a successful and better attorney. They do not have to follow your advice. They only have to appreciate and respect what you are saying. At that point, all decisions are informed and you have provided the utmost level of representation to your client. (As a sidenote, I have always enjoyed the double standard of the "no guaranty" approach. Attorneys know that they cannot guaranty a win. However, many are so negative that when speaking to a client, they in essence guaranty a loss. I assure you that client will hire me over them. Every case has good and bad, so quit guaranteeing either way, especially the losses.)

In addition, I believe that you should start with any negative issues when conversing with your clients, then immediately switch to the positive. The positive should also be *longer.* I had a client who called to complain about an upcoming hearing with another lawyer in our office—he was worried because the attorney told him it was a long shot. The attorney offered no positive enforcement. All he had to do was tell the client was that winning the case was a long shot, but "Here is what we are going to do . . . and this is what the positive facts are . . ." Clients want a positive attorney. A client was driving me crazy over his concern—our attorney lost control of the client due to his attitude and his failure to communicate better. Maintaining control of the client will make you a better attorney.

When you are confident, if anything, your client will put his or her faith in you and other attorneys will be more respectful of you. Who do you fear in a legal challenge? Do you really want the client second-guessing you because you are so negative and scared? Of course not. You would then have to spend time rebuilding the relationship.

Everyone tells me that I am too aggressive . . . *except* my clients. (I'm not saying being aggressive is better or not, but it does work.) No client has ever asked for the dachshund or poodle attorney—they want the bulldog. You need to be a fighter for your clients. The point is that once the client thinks of you as the end-all, your suggestions and instructions will be followed. Without confidence, you cannot bring clients who have unrealistic goals back to reality because they will not trust you and they will second-guess your decisions, your management, and your ability to provide great legal services. Your self-confidence builds confidence in your clients, and will make opponents second-guess themselves, as well.

Additionally, do not let the client know if you have no idea what the answer is. Instead, you could say something like "Now clearly, there are many different variables that apply and that will determine our strategy." If you say nothing, but say it in a positive and confident manner, you still have client control and confidence. For example, you might say, "Your case could go in a number of directions: this way, this way, or this way.

But before we go, I need to review everything to determine which avenue we should follow." You could tell the client "I do not know anything," which may be the case, but that will make you look weak, so why not at least create the impression that you are confident in the task before you?

I was a confirming attorney in my younger days. I would give straightforward advice, and then run down the hall to confirm or to see if I was remotely close. On a number of occasions, I had to run right back to call the client to suggest the law had changed, so my initial conclusion needed to change. Nonetheless, the client still thought of me as knowledgeable and as a solid attorney rather than someone who simply said, "I don't know the answer."

As a last tip on confidence, never get bullied. For the first two and a half years that I was practicing, I constantly heard the old guard saying things like, "I have been practicing for thirty years, and I have never seen this." I felt insecure at times until I realized some of these older attorneys just accepted the status quo and had never seen any new theories. Nobody knows everything, but if you are an attorney, your goal should be to know it all. Do not lose confidence for any reason. Also, when you hear those comments, it is a positive in any respect because you are thinking *independently*, and even if you're wrong, you gave it a shot. Do not let some eighty-five-year-old attorney belittle you when you are trying. (One response you can use after you gain real confidence through experience is something like "I just took the bar, and this is how we do it nowadays.")

A confident attorney can control everyone better. Your clients will be managed better, make sounder decisions, and defer to you more, which is how it should be as you are providing the guidance. On top of it, a confident and aggressive attorney also has a psychological edge—the other side knows you will not stop. The point is, this approach gives you more client control and an advantage in any situation, making you a better attorney.

CONNECT WITH YOUR CLIENTS

This is one of the most important focuses of generating business with new clients. A connection with an existing client is also an ultimate goal of a practice. If you develop a connection, a client not only looks to you as a lawyer but as a friend in need. Find something you have in common, just as you did with your interviewer in Section I, as this helps further the attorney-client relationship. You are no longer just their lawyer, but someone they trust.

DETERMINE YOUR CLIENT'S GOALS AND CONCERNS

Figure out the client's goals and concerns. I sometimes find myself in the middle of a fifteen-minute conversation when I finally ask the client, "What do you want?" The key to understanding the matter is to have an end goal in sight. The goals may change, but at least you have your reminder. If the client's goal is outrageous or, at a minimum, different from what you think the goal is, you have a problem.

Once you determine the goal, write it down. This will help you stay on track so you can always try to figure out how to achieve that goal. Do not be reactive, be proactive. Creating a calculated plan will help you be the first to the finish line.

Start analyzing any concerns, and make a *written* checklist. After I am initially retained by a client, I immediately type up a checklist of my client concerns, including questions (e.g., who, what, etc.), goals, specific facts, concerns, and issues (e.g., money). It is brief and even employs one-word line items (e.g., money). The key to the checklist is that it reminds me of the client and the particulars of the case, so I can always stay *focused* on what the client wants while remembering their personal situation and/or other pertinent facts. Keep it accessible in the file; if you do not remember certain things about the file, review it. You would be surprised by how much memory is triggered from those simple line items.

USE YOUR TIME WISELY

Make the most of your time, or as I call it, billable time. It is better to do work than to do nothing. This is billable time. A tremendous number of hours are always wasted. Do you listen to talk radio? If so, no more radio—you have an average of fifteen to forty minutes in the car every day to bill and get phone calls or other work done. Why waste your time? I always carry a Dictaphone (you could also use an application on your phone) to prepare e-mails and documents for my assistant to produce when I get in, or even better, by the time I get in. I e-mail her messages in draft form, which are then ready for my review upon my arrival. The point is, this time can help you get caught up with your work or, at a minimum, create billable hours.

I still cannot believe that I have to tell people this, but I will never forget asking a first-year associate on a Tuesday morning if he had returned a Monday night call at 5:40 p.m. He explained that he'd just arrived and it was the first thing he was going to do that morning. We talked about his drive and all the interesting sports updates, and then I asked him if that was the best use of this time. Why not get the phone call out of the way, *then* call me to report. That would be proactive (and more importantly, I would not have had to spend four minutes of my time tracking him down to remind him of the assignment). What a novel idea! (Except, it's actually pretty basic.)

When you have a minute, at any time, do something proactive. Get a phone call out of the way that is due the next day. Give an update. You will be surprised how much time you have that you are not using for any work-related purpose. If you have forty minutes in the car, dictate a pleading or an agreement and/or letter. Do not come in and tell me your assignment is behind in the same sentence wherein you talk about the discussion on ESPN radio that morning.

ALWAYS BILL ACCURATELY

Doing this is actually quite simple and starts with one clear concept: write down your time. You need to make sure you bill. Use the "free time" mentioned above to get caught up. If you are making billable time, then write it down. Do not fall behind by more than four hours and always think back to the last three or four hours to make sure nothing was missed. Billing is how you and your firm get paid, and you were hired for that purpose.

Now that you have written down your time, you need to bill the client and be cognizant of that bill. *Do not be afraid to bill.* If you are concerned you will offend the client by sending a bill, call me! I will hire you because I would love to employ an attorney who wants to work for free. Think of it this way: if you do not want to charge the client by sending a bill, then you are better off not having the client. We all have clients who we walk on eggshells around, and there are different ways of handling them, but do not be afraid to ask to get paid for work you did. Also, for the younger lawyers, you need to bill in order to keep your job. I find that all attorneys (including me) are reluctant to bill at certain times, and it irritates me when I feel that way. Why shouldn't the client pay? I was there for them and I did great work. Why shouldn't I be compensated in full? In summary, if you are too afraid to bill, then you may want to consider working in a tollbooth.

Make sure you review your bills carefully. If you spent too much time on something, give the client a courtesy discount to keep your time within market rates. Let them see the discount, as well. Sometimes it is easier to discount the bill because certain clients will always ask for a discount. The nerve? Not really. They feel like they are exceptional clients and that they are entitled to a little extra. Truthfully, if the discount requested is not offensive, sometimes it is better to just provide it—losing

$1,500 on a larger bill may be more beneficial in the long run than standing firm on the bill discussion for a few hours when dealing with the client. Sometimes when I discount a bill, I also give a reason and explanation (e.g., I might tell the client it is because the deal fell apart and I feel bad for them).

Here is another novel idea: ask for a retainer. In connection with this, ask for an engagement letter to be executed. This is not 2005. People will use you, make demands of you, and then give every reason not to pay you. Get the money first. You also need to determine the amount of the retainer. Most firms will have set amounts, so work off those numbers. Do not fall behind on the retainer. Keep an eye on the monies in escrow. Falling behind a little is a common practice, but if you fall behind too much, the snowball effect can take place. In the transactional world, all of a sudden, you are working and hoping the deal closes so you can get paid. It is a major problem if the deal falls apart, as most clients despise paying bills on deals that did not go through. Billing correctly and keeping an eye on the retainer will help you maintain leverage in the relationship.

Reminder: do not forget or be afraid to ask for a retainer to be replenished or for an outstanding bill to be paid.

Also, do not forget credit cards. It's an easy way to get paid.

Lastly, you need to make sure you know *how* to bill. There is always a cost reward, so be mindful of the time you spend on billing. If it far exceeds any potential benefit, you need to bring the client up to speed immediately, or they will question why they owe $35,000 on a $25,000 claim.

Clients like to see bills after a positive result (at least, this is the best time to send them). Billing for chickenshit with no results will create an angry client. As a tip, try to think how you would feel receiving a bill for services rendered without any results or outcome. Would you be happy? Timing helps.

USING FORMS EFFECTIVELY

It is always good to have forms. Forms help with the structure, but you need to do the work *first*. You need to analyze yourself, and *then* look to the forms.

Do not be a form attorney who simply regurgitates. You need to learn to develop your own thoughts, because if you are spoon-fed information by simply reviewing the forms, you will not grow as an attorney.

Instead, try on your own and fail miserably, which will help you make progress along the way. After the initial analysis is done and the notes are written, the assignment is to be drafted without—and I repeat, *without*—looking at the forms. Your independent analysis will help you generate independent ideas, and it will also humble you when you compare your own work to the forms. This will help your baby brain learn to think independently and grow. (As it turns out, when you start practicing law, as I indicated earlier, you have very little ability to analyze.) Those who have depended entirely on forms have limited their own growth. If you rely entirely on past work, you will never make progress. You will start to think better when you utilize this method.

After you become experienced, try to build your own forms. My forms were created by combining the forms of three other attorneys. Now they include my independent thoughts and I have created a better and more comprehensive form. Also, in the form itself, you can leave notes in **bold** to remind yourself of the details (e.g., "This dealt with a construction loan").

You also have to *update* your forms regularly, not simply rely on what you have. If you see something new, you need to spend five minutes updating your forms. Sometimes I simply add in another reminder in the form itself, so no work is done until that form is used again (e.g., Reminder: Add language to address . . .).

Finally, but most simply, forms are no good if you cannot find them. I use a database by category. I also use some keywords in the title of the document so it is easier to search for and find in my database. For instance, I have numerous commercial lease forms in my "Lease" database. My main go-to lease for a landlord is named "Landlord This Is It" with the date; for a tenant, the name is "Tenant This Is It" with the date. Another is called "Landlord Buildout Language." The key is to find the header that will bring up the form as quickly as possible several years down the road.

COMPLETE AN ANALYSIS OF THE PLAYERS

The entire practice of law is a psychological game. To succeed, you must understand and analyze all the participants. The more you understand, the better you will become at being proactive and having a firmer grasp on how to deal with each issue. As you recall, we analyzed the problem earlier. Now we need to understand the financial aspects of everyone involved, as well as identify the players.

1. Perform cost-reward analysis. Try to figure out the cost of doing the work (estimate) and make sure you and the client are in the same ballpark. Everyone is afraid to talk about money. Why? Because you think you will scare the client away. You might think, "It's better not to accept an engagement than to have an upset client because they spent thirty times more than what they would have achieved on their best day." You need to get a grasp on this concept.

Lawyers are so busy practicing law that they forget every matter is a *business_transaction* to the client. The sooner you understand this, the quicker you can start with the client or move on. For example, I get numerous phone calls from referrals. They go something like this:

Client: Mr. Cohen, I am getting evicted.

Me: Why?

Client: I did not pay my rent.

Me, in my brain: Then you surely will not be able to pay my bill.

Me, actual response: Why don't you come in with your lease and consultation fee of $500? Otherwise, I'm not sure I can help.

Click.

Me: I guess they thought I would do this pro bono.

I understand that I wasted five minutes of my time for a matter that was not going anywhere. It used to be worse—I would talk for thirty minutes and then mention the retainer.

On the reverse side, if you have clients with a lot of money who have a small "principle-oriented" dispute, you need to be careful of watching the fees. This is not a churn the fee file.

The point I am making is that every matter must be analyzed from a cost standpoint and with regard to the risk involved. For example, if your TV is broken and it costs $2,000 to fix but you can buy a new, upgraded television for $1,500, which deal do you take? That is what the client is thinking (the lone exception of being divorce cases, where emotion drives everything). Paying $75,000 to recover $50,000 does not work. It is your job to make things clear to the client, try to keep the matter under control, and keep them informed.

2. Assess your client's personal situation. It's important to understand the client and their personal situation. Do they have money? What is the timeline? Is this a hands-on client? Do they need some extra attention? For example, I represent certain builders who wake up at 4:00 a.m. When I call them at 4:30 a.m. they feel important, and they enjoy getting an update first thing in the morning. I like it, too, because I just knocked off one phone call. Understanding the specifics of a client is just as important as handling the matter, because it helps you learn how best to deal with them.

The financial ability of your client to pay is also important.

If they cannot pay, you have an issue. Sometimes the financial situation of *either* the client or the attorney dictates how you come out of the gate entirely. For example, if you serve a lawsuit with tremendous discovery, your client has to pay, but your opposition will get a feel for how this matter will be handled—or at least believe that the matter will be costly and perhaps push them into a more reasonable state.

You must understand that there are issues like this on every matter, and you are not simply a robot that should take in a case, charge a file, lose a client, and develop a terrible reputation.

In summary, do not just practice law, practice business. Always remember the economics of the matter and the personal situation of the client, as well as any other business factors and considerations that actually control the client. Understand the business. Litigation attorneys should focus on this, as I find that many of you are oblivious to the concept of business. (This is often revealed during mediation when I tell opposing parties what they will spend on a full-fledged lawsuit. Why the other attorneys did not discuss this with their clients is beyond me.)

3. Identify the other attorneys. This is also part of the analysis because you can't know how to deal with a fellow attorney if you don't know anything about him or her. Who is the attorney on the other side? Do you know them? Do you have mutual friends? Are they tough? Nice? Older than you? A lot older than you? Do they litigate? The analysis goes on and on. Think of it like playing a competitive sport. If you know your opponent's weaknesses and strengths, it is easier to win or at least control the play.

I had a deal with a sole practitioner who did not litigate. On a number of issues, I kept telling him that we were trying to avoid litigation. Imagine how he was feeling. In the back of his mind, he knew he would have to work harder to get the deal done or else he was going to lose the matter to an outside firm. Now you control him as you can already predict what is going through his mind.

Here are some general observations of stereotypical attorneys and methods you can utilize to deal with them:

A. **Attorneys with fifty years of experience** on their way out of the practice and looking forward to retirement who remind you how much they know and how long they've practiced. This is a tough one. I always try to act like the naive grandson who doesn't know anything. I often ask, "Can you help me out?" Being nice always got me far when dealing with this type of attorney. If they do not do something you like, ask with a leading question so they come up with the conclusion you want. For example, "Perhaps if we did it this way, that would work? Hopefully you agree." With their experience, they also deserve respect.

B. **Pompous, arrogant attorneys** with more experience but who are not on the way out like the fifty-plusers. Always remember, arrogant attorneys are *second-tier* attorneys. Anyone who is rude to younger lawyers is pathetic. I have always brought it out in the open by asking, "Is there any particular reason you are so rude to me?" Put them on the spot. Remind them of your place by saying something like "I am not sure what I know as I am new at this." Sometimes I even ask, "What would you do?" This at least helps in avoiding more confrontation as they now are reminded that you are not there to fight (maybe a little) or be abused, but you are just trying to be a better lawyer.

C. **Certain big firm attorneys with big egos.** (This is not every attorney at big firms, naturally, but the ones who believe because they are at a big firm, they are superior. In fact, this only makes them superior douchebags). I just try to remind them that their firm name means nothing. They did well in law school and take tests well. Do not be afraid or intimidated because someone is at a larger firm than yours or because someone is a specialist. Oftentimes, nowadays, I get a new perspective from a young attorney who is thinking unconventionally.

Knowing whether other attorneys are struggling financially is also important. This is a tough one to pick up on, but when there are signs, such as them complaining about their lack of business, you should take these factors into consideration to help your client (e.g., an insurance defense lawyer may know that the other attorney is struggling, so he pushes the matter to trial to force the other's hand, as that would be costly). I believe this is more prevalent in the personal-injury world, so personal-injury attorneys, make sure you do not create this impression. Let everyone know, regardless of if you *want* to try a case, that you are not *afraid* to do so.

Once you know all about the other lawyers involved, try to find the common connection with them. (Are you sensing a theme?) At the end of the day, a connection with the opposition puts you in a better light and brings their guard down.

3. Know who the judge is. Do not forget the trier of the case. Does the judge like you? Always take into account your relationship or your firm's relationship with the judge, and, just as important, the other attorney's relationship with the judge. When Cohen the Jewish Attorney walks into the courtroom in Hillbillyville, for example, and finds out the judge went fishing with the opposing attorney, he needs to strategize differently. Move to recuse? Good luck! (Get someone local to stand with you.)

In addition, don't forget the following:

A. Focus on what matters to them and do not sweat the small things. They make the decisions.
B. Do not be annoying.
C. Learn their preferences.
D. Attend functions that judges attend and get to know them.
E. Look them up on the Internet. Learn about them (e.g., kids, colleges, etc.), just as you would for the other attorney.

F. Try to create a connection.

G. Do not be a lawyer who fights everything. Be a *good* lawyer who fights for important matters.

Remember: the more you know and think about both a matter and the players, the better you can prepare to achieve the best results. Do not forget to apply the who, what, where, when, why, and how questions to the case, your client, the opposition, the other attorney, and the judge. In the world of law, which is basically a game of chess, if you know all the players and their financial situations, you will be psychologically ahead of everyone else and you will achieve the best results.

NEGOTIATIONS (PSYCHOLOGICAL)

It is important that every lawyer learns how to negotiate and how to prepare for the negotiation.

1. Determine the client's goals. Once you know the client's goals, always remind the client that attaining their goals is your top priority (and it's why you were hired!).

2. Analyze the opponent. What do you anticipate their goals are? Go through the strengths and weaknesses of each side. Understand your client's finances, the opposition's finances, the other attorney, and the judges, as this is how you prepare for negotiations. As you would with the case, analyze everything.

3. Learn when to flex but *never* draw a line in the sand. That is, unless you will *never ever* cross it. When an attorney gives me an ultimatum and then changes his terms, I already own him. "Nothing less than $100,000". You mean to tell me if I offer $99,999, that won't work? No more credibility.

4. Never act like you *want* to settle. Some attorneys simply let everyone know when they feel a case is weak (usually they communicate this even in their body language), but that doesn't inspire much confidence in your client.

5. Acting unreasonable is not always bad. If you consistently act unreasonably, sometimes that will affect the other side. They begin to accommodate as they see how ridiculous your position is. Even sometimes acting unreasonably exudes extra confidence.

6. Do not eat or go to the bathroom before a sit-down mediation. When you make your initial presentation, you should be irritable and angry. This will make the other side question how bad it could get for them. I am not kidding. (In fact, I am angry writing this right now as I have to go to the bathroom.)

7. If the law is on your side, use it. If it is not, tell the client you do not care if that is the case, and you expect the equitable result will be obtained.

8. If possible, discuss strategies with another attorney in your office. It is always best to get a second perspective when dealing with negotiations.

9. Keep the negotiations going as long as you can. You need to return to the table continuously while standing firm. If one of the spouses or parties is difficult, I will get back to him or her. Perhaps you are the difficult one. Sometimes an attorney needs justification, so blame needs to be placed either on you or on the client. This always justifies going back to the table to keep negotiations from ending.

There is no absolute set of rules for negotiations because they change as you deal with different situations and parties. However, I do believe the analysis above is important in order to be successful in this aspect of practicing law.

MAINTAIN A SOLID REPUTATION

Your reputation is all you have to show clients, peers, judges, and others. Here are some tips to remind you how you can at least maintain a solid reputation in the legal community (and also, the local).

1. Do not "over-lawyer." This is especially prevalent with judges, as discussed previously. Do not be the nuisance who offends people.

2. Pick your battles. You do not want to be the person who irritates every attorney. Use discretion to get things done in the best, most efficient manner for your client. If something does not matter, move on. Plus, there is no reason to bill for chickenshit, as the client will get angry.

3. Never act unprofessionally or spitefully. Nobody will ever practice law and never have issues with another attorney. There will always be issues, but it is up to you to do everything on the up and up to preserve your reputation. It is okay if people do not to like you because you represented someone well; it is not okay if the reason they do not like you is because you perform underhanded nonsense to make their lives difficult.

4. Do not yell at people. This is disrespectful, and, admittedly, an area that I hope to get better with myself. I achieve much better results when I am calm and collected than when I lose it. It is okay to be upset with the other attorney—or whomever—but yelling is not the answer.

5. Never act like you know something when you do not. If you are trying to look good, and your cover-up is discovered, the other attorney will always remember you, and will remind other attorneys that you bluffed.

I still remember when I was younger, I did not understand something in a contract, so I crossed it out. (I'd told the attorney the reason I asked to take it out was because I did not understand it.) The other attorney continually argued with me, claiming "It is standard language and it is never removed." After I took the time to figure it out, it turned out the language was more beneficial to him if it stayed in, and this attorney was actually arguing against my own ignorance. To this day, I remember him. The point is, if you do not know, you can tell the other attorney (it usually creates a better connection with them, as they will feel honored that you would ask them), but do not act like you know something you do not or you will be the main character of many stories like the jackass above (at least I did not say his name).

6. Attorneys talk, so be careful how you act. When I deal with an attorney who is very rude, I make it a point to tell every attorney I know about how they acted. (I also forward on nasty e-mails, as I referenced earlier.) Now that attorney's reputation has been adjusted due to the rude manner in which he acted toward me. There are consequences to being rude and disrespectful.

7. Always thank the other attorney and their assistants when done. Completing a matter or case is a joint effort and everyone should be thankful for the help of the other parties.

SUMMARY

Now that you understand the relationship, you can really practice law—or at least you have a good idea of how to do it better. I am hopeful you will follow the directions above; if so, you will become a better person and a better attorney. You will also be held in a higher regard by others, and you can better appreciate the attorney-client relationship. It's too bad they did not teach this in law school.

Chapter Two

Additional Tips to Becoming a Great Lawyer

There is always more you can do to be a successful attorney. In fact, there is always more you *should* do.

1. Wake up early. If you are not a morning person, *change*. (Actually, this should have started in law school!) If you get to the office at 6:30 a.m., that hour and a half before the real start time is the equivalent of three hours during normal business hours. People try to convince me it is the same at night, but I disagree, as our brains are fried and so the output is not as great. If you wake up at 5:00 a.m., rather than turning back to sleep for an hour, get out of bed and get moving. If you have children, this free or peaceful time is actually wonderful. Do not waste four hours a week tossing and turning when it can be extra production or, even better, billable time. Plus, have an ego about being the first in to work. Nothing makes me happier than when an associate is in fifteen minutes earlier than me.

2. Think about the case on the weekend or at home. Everyone needs to analyze outside of the daily grind. You are constantly being interrupted by noise and distractions—other phone calls, e-mails, lawyers, other clients, et al. You need private time on the weekends, or early or late, when nothing can distract you from thinking through the issues.

3. When tired, get refreshed. This can be ten-minute nap (which you have to hide from the boss) or a quick drive to the store for coffee. The nap, unfortunately, is not billable, but the drive is if you are on the phone. Sitting at a desk will drain you, so all you need is a brief change of scenery and you will feel better, even if you are still working. I schedule all my large and long meetings late in the day, because afterward I am drained. It's a terrible feeling to be that drained at 10:30 a.m.

4. Never take the client for granted. I find that most attorneys, including myself, think we are the end-all for our clients. Most attorneys (except for myself, naturally) are wrong about this. You see, practicing law is not that hard if you care about the client and actually *try* to achieve the best results for them. How many times does a lawyer do something spectacular that very few others could do? Maybe once a year. Do not forget this. You need to appreciate the client—they do not need to appreciate you. If you follow this creed, you will maintain the relationship better. If you do not, you will take the client for granted, and you should not be surprised when they fire you and hire somebody else. There are a million other attorneys out there who can do exactly what you can do.

5. Give 100 percent. Always. Make your life more difficult by always being an overzealous attorney rather than a moderate attorney. Everything you do should always be about representing the client 100 percent, without compromise. The second you do not give 100 percent, you become average and you are doing a disservice to your client.

6. Do not be afraid of malpractice lawsuits. If you start thinking you are going to make a mistake, you will not win.

7. Do not cross the line into unlawful acts. When your stomach feels weird or you know something is too close, stop before you cross the line. If you find yourself asking, "Is this too far over or is it on the line?" then you *are* over the line and it is time to get out or go back. We all want results and business, but nothing is worth a license revocation. Always do the right thing. When you break the rules, you lose. Have integrity.

I had a deal once where the client decided in the twenty-third hour that he did not want to play by the rules. We talked about it. I told him I could not compromise. In fact, I said good-bye and good luck, and I put the bill in the mail. Incredibly enough, weeks later he changed his course and my initial message was relayed to his partners (whom I didn't know). Now they want me to represent them on all their matters. A dollar now is not worth it down the road if it compromises your ethics and jeopardizes your license. Your reputation should speak for you.

8. Get your e-mails on your phone. Most people already do this, but I remind the older generations that this speeds up *response* time. Fast and accessible attorneys are the best.

9. Always carry a Dictaphone. Dictate ideas (e.g., "Issue—just saw this in the paper—does it apply to our case? Make a note to call someone to discuss"). You also need to learn to dictate on a Dictaphone; it will take a few months to master.

10. Get board certified. Now you are an expert in your field. Older attorneys will no longer question you. Clients now respect you. Looking good on paper gives your reputation a head start.

11. Join groups, committees, et al. and be active with the bar association and/or charities. Meeting the players (i.e., other attorneys and judges) and developing connections helps with the analysis of any matter.

12. Write down every phone call you need to return on a legal pad and cross off the name after speaking. Check it if you left message. This way, you will never forget to return a call. A legal pad is easy to carry around, as well. An unreturned phone call equals an angry client.

13. Get organized. Create piles and a to-do list. (This also helps with billing.) Figure out the best mechanism that works for you. Ask other attorneys how they set up their offices. I even have a follow-up networking pile.

Some lists I would suggest are the following:

A. Case lists
B. To-do lists
C. Awaiting reply lists on matters
D. New matter / follow-up lists
E. Potential client list
F. Miscellaneous list

In the early stages, it is best to watch and learn from older, experienced attorneys who have certain mechanisms for staying organized. As you develop as an attorney, you will learn to refine everything so it works best for you.

14. Before you leave every day, look to see what is due and upcoming the next day. Also, on Monday mornings, have your assistant confirm your lunches and appointments for the week.

15. Do not forget the basic rules from the other parts of this book.

A. We always exceed the goals given to us or that we create.
B. We remember that we are nothing and are lucky to be there.

C. We approach everything by first asking who, what, where, when, why, and how.

D. Weekends are partially for the firm (those days count when determining turnaround time).

16. Work well with your assistant. You each need the other. You should complement each other; nobody works *for* someone, so working *with* each other is the goal. Learn each other's weaknesses and strengths, and use them to break up the assignments. For example, when I am in a bad mood, my letters tend to get longer and ramble on, so my assistant always makes sure that I review them when I have calmed down. If you and your assistant work well together, you will be so much more productive. Never treat your assistant with any less respect than you expect to receive. I cannot stress enough how much a good assistant will better your business. I should know—I have had at least thirty-five of them; however, as of now, my present assistant/lifeblood and I have been together for over eight years, give or take a baby or two of maternity leave. My work product and quantity continually increases.

Your coworkers, staff, and/or assistants should *want* to work with you, and they should like you. I am impatient; it is my worst quality (or at least tied for worst). At the same time, my support staff knows that I will kill for them and would never throw them under the bus. If you enjoy your job, particularly the people you work with, you will obtain better results from positive attitudes, which enhances your practice and services to clients.

17. How you dress is very important. Just as you should with an interview, you should look professional. People look up to you as an attorney.

18. Think before you respond. Every response you make, whether returning a call or an e-mail, needs to be calculated.

19. Confer with other attorneys. I believe transactional attorneys understand business, while litigation attorneys understand judges. It is always good to confer with attorneys outside your area of practice to attain perspective on different situations.

20. Control your clients. You must control your clients (to an extent) to obtain the best results. Do not let them override you, as everyone loses in that case.

21. Dominate the room. Be the one in charge, the one in command. If you are, people listen to you and you will obtain the desired results. This will not happen in the beginning, but it should be your goal.

22. Remind your client that he or she is not alone. No matter what your client is spending for your services, the other side is spending money, as well (hopefully more), and it is important to remind your client of that fact. This is also something to remind your client of when they are upset about the bill or a delay of their case.

23. Always carry a legal pad in your car and to every meeting. You will look like an attorney. And if you need to call someone, you'll be able to write it down on a list so you do not forget.

24. Turn complaints into positives. Surprisingly enough, sometimes statements like "I am sorry," "I will address it," and "I want to be your go-to person" really work, and they might just help turn a bad experience into one that strengthens your relationship with your client.

25. Plan around your vacations or being out of the office. If you're going to be out of the office or on vacation, give your assistant some assignments before you leave so the work/drafts are done when you return. Also, when you're back from vacation, go in *the day before* to get caught up. For every day you are out, you will need at least one to one and a half hours to get caught up and get organized. You will feel good that night when everything is done and even better when you officially return to work the next day.

I also always add an extra day to my e-mail saying I am out of town so nobody knows I am in the first day I return.

26. Put your cell number on your e-mails. Clients should be able to reach you on your cell phone. It is very irritating for me to receive a call from a client over the weekend because they cannot reach an associate. I am not sure why I should have to field calls over the weekend on matters they are working on. It's simple: the client should have their number.

27. Brainstorm with other attorneys you know. I even attend a monthly group breakfast to discuss issues. I also meet an attorney friend for a meal once every few months to talk about more particular issues and ideas. It is amazing how similar the issues, ideas, and problems we face are, but how different our approaches can be. This can also lead to business generation.

28. As with everything, develop your style, but watch other people, as well. Most people do things in their own unique way, so pick and choose. If you are fortunate enough to have experienced people around you, absorb any information you can from all of them and decide what works best *for you*.

29. If you manage people in your office, go see them. Let them know you care. If you do not, you probably should not be there. Better people means better representation of a client.

30. Always look at your phone and computer for e-mails *once every forty-five minutes* **at a minimum.** Sometimes punching out a few yes or no answers (if applicable) on the computer saves you valuable time later. Plus, the faster the response, the better you look to the client. The elevator is a good time for this, as well (but do not forget to write down your time).

31. Enjoy and appreciate practicing and serving your clients. Nothing is better than something productive that helps someone.

THINGS TO AVOID IF YOU WANT TO BE A GREAT LAWYER

Just as there are things you should always do if you want to succeed as an attorney, there are things that you must *never* do, too.

1. Never sell out your assistant or anyone in your office. You need to accept responsibility for any poor work they do. They report to you and a client does not care—they will blame you anyway.

2. Do not cover up mistakes. Face them. They will eventually come out and it is best to have told the client, not just let them find out.

3. Try not to be late to any meetings outside of the office. This is impossible, I know, but it is a good practice to follow.

4. Don't expect vacations to be 100 percent vacations. There might be some time to do a little work. When I went on a trip with a few friends, they set aside one hour a day to prospect and generate business—there was even a contest to do it. If you get a new matter for your efforts, your vacation will pay for itself.

5. Do not lie. If a person is honest and fair, I have nothing bad to say, but a bad reputation is impossible to undo.

6. Never send an e-mail or letter when angry or upset. Calm down, tone down, and then send it out. Remember: you can never get an e-mail back and print is forever.

7. Firing a client is okay, but do not fire a client because they annoy you. If your client is a crook, drop them, but do not let your emotions get the best of you. Sometimes a client will drone on and with the pressure, you may reach your boiling point. Hold it in. Do not get frustrated and take it out on the client. You could lose money.

8. Do not have your assistant set up your voice mail. You want to have your own voice on your outgoing message. When an assistant does your messages, you come off as arrogant and egotistical—the type of attorney that you do not want to be.

9. Do not sell yourself out to make money. When I see lawyers take on representation of bad people, just to make a dollar, I know that they are lesser attorneys for compromising their values. I used to do it when I was young, but now I have the luxury of rejecting this type of client. In the end, the bad people/clients will end up draining you, and oftentimes attempt to bring you into their world where morals do not exist – avoid them.

SPECIALIZED TIPS ON BEING A TRANSACTIONAL ATTORNEY

While the next part of this section specifically deals with my mentality as a *transactional attorney*, I am hopeful that litigators et al. can apply some of this information and approach to their practices, too.

The golden rule of transactional work is to "get it done." The client has property to buy or sell, and in over 99 percent of all situations, no legal language, no tempers, and especially no other attorneys should ever get in the way. If you do not have a contract and closing, you do not have anything.

1. Remember what is important and do what you can to get there. You must have discretion to realize what is and is not necessary.

2. Do not be afraid of requesting changes to any offer. If you are scared, your client will be scared and the deal may not get done. It is very rare that a bullet point (major point of a deal) does not get worked out on a deal. Do not forget, if it is something very necessary to you, the opposing side should understand, as well.

3. If a deal cannot be completed, it should be because it is the client's decision, not your decision. I deal with so many "nervous attorneys" that scare their clients to the point that they walk away from deals for ridiculous reasons (and I mean *ridiculous*). The term "deal killer" is a kiss of death in the industry, and you will lose referrals because most of the people referring a deal to you only get paid if the deal closes. I also deal with attorneys whose egos compromise transactions, as they are attempting to flex their muscles to act tough—it is a terrible mechanism. Just remember, it is the client doing the deal, not you, so do not let your personal feelings or your ego get in the way.

If a deal does not get done because of you, not your client, it may be the last with that client.

SPECIALIZED TIPS ON BEING A LITIGATOR

As with the previous subsection, these may be specialized tips, but they are also somewhat universal. When presenting, arguing, or making a case to anyone, there are several things you'll want to do:

1. Present like you are talking to a friend. Do not get caught up in the whole legal thing. Every time I go to court, or get involved with moot court, one painful situation always arises. One or both the lawyers focus so much on the law (e.g., cases, statutes, history) that they forget to focus on the obvious part of the matter. In every case, there is always a point that is obvious from your standpoint, so make that the focus and the basis for the argument. Ever hear a long-winded story about someone, and you immediately know what they did wrong? You know because it is obvious. It is the same effect here.

2. Do not make everything an argument. The small stuff usually is just small, and it does not matter. This also takes away from your ability to focus on the big stuff or the obvious.

3. Do not get nervous. If you lose a case and you did your best—that is all you can do. No reason to be nervous.

4. Equity and nonlegal facts matter. People always want the "good team" or "right person" to win, regardless of the law. Keep that in mind when deciding how you want to practice.

SUMMARY

The Do's and Don't's in this chapter—should you follow them, this will help you improve your effectiveness and efficiency, whether you are a litigator, transactional attorney, or otherwise.

SECTION III

GENERATING BUSINESS

Now that you have grasped tips on how to be a great lawyer, you are waiting in your office for your next assignment. The problem is, even if you are the greatest lawyer of all time, without any business, you are one of the masses. This next section will focus on business generation, teaching you how to get clients from every single approach imaginable. If you leave this book with one idea from this section, it will translate into money in your pocket. (It sounds like an infomercial, I know.) Imagine if you use all of them. *This is the most important part of this book and of the practice of law.* It is what allows you to practice, make a living, and thrive.

Generating business is my area of expertise. From my first real estate client to my present practice, I have employed my independent approach to generating business and have built a voluminous practice over twenty years.

Practicing law in the manner described in Section II is really not that difficult. Even if you master it though, it is only half of the equation. The other half, and the most important half, is the business generation. If you bring in business, you are unique.

I do love the law, but just as much, I love bringing in a client to help them. Most lawyers focus on the practice side, which is important, but if you want to be independent and self-sufficient, you need to adhere to the following guidelines. They will help distinguish you from the rest.

This information or focus is not taught in law school (or anywhere else as far as I know), and some tips may be generic. I assure you, in the legal world, these ideas *work*. Plus, as you will see, some are fun. In fact, if you employ them, I expect you will enjoy the practice more, as you are not only helping build your own practice, you are helping others develop business.

Before we get into tips and ideas on how to generate business, we need to find out what type of lawyer you are.

Chapter One

Different Types of Lawyers

To state it simply, there are Minders, Grinders, and Finders. The goal is to excel in all three styles, but so many people forget the third category, Finder, which truly is the most important.

What are Minder attorneys? The Minders are the smart guys, the people who always did very well on tests, had a better grasp of what the professors were looking for, and sometimes spoke the most in law school. (Sometimes, their questions were not really questions, but thoughts disguised as questions to remind everyone how smart they were.) They are extremely analytical, oftentimes going steps beyond what you did in your preparation, law review, or clerking at large firms . . . You get the point. In summary, they were smarter than most, including me.

How are these individuals faring in the real world? Most have left the practice of law and gone on to do very well in other professions, such as investments. They can analyze a fact well, but they may be lacking in two areas: (1) application to the real world, and (2) connection to the clients. They also forget to apply the basic points of practicing law referenced in Section II.

Not everything is simply the law; there are other factors on every matter that must be analyzed, as previously discussed, and simply regurgitating facts does not capture or keep a client.

Minders are great workers to a point, as they understand the law and, short of additional considerations on a case, connect with other intelligent people. They bill up to what they are told (following instructions to a tee is a common trait), write well, and often have more strengths than weaknesses. Minders are perfect employees, as they have nowhere else to go. They are easily replaced by other Minders. Sorry to inform you Minders of this, but unless you are also a Finder, you are part of an overpopulated group of lawyers who have neither business nor a book of business. You are expendable. The fact is, you can be the best attorney around (and you may be if you truly understand the points in Section II), but without business, you are a stay-at-home mom or dad.

What are Grinder attorneys? These are the fighters. They are not as smart, but they can will their way through. They cannot analyze like a Minder, but they can apply the practical issues better. (Section II will help improve your analysis from an intellectual point of view so you are not just touching the surface of the issue.) Strengths are, again, the work ethic and desire to get a matter done. Your weakness is that sometimes you are not as smart as the others at the table. (Again, I stress, read Section II.) The Grinder will work extra hard, but will bill more hours to get something done.

Your goal as an attorney is to be the best of both Minders and Grinders. Although I cannot teach you to be smarter by

4L – THE CLASS NEVER TAUGHT IN LAW SCHOOL | 87

reading, following the steps outlined in Section II will improve your traits so that you are the best Minder and Grinder you can be.

Minders and Grinders, if you stop there, are perfect employees for *a firm*. You can work well, you keep and maintain business as you do good work, but as I indicated above, you have nowhere else to go and you are *easily replaceable* (there are hundreds of thousands of Minders and Grinders). This will always be the case unless you are also a Finder.

What are Finder attorneys? Finders are the lawyers who bring in the business. They know how to connect with clients and/or potential clients. As smart as the Minders, they are very good at their niche, creating business *and money.* The tough part of Finders is they realize the business element to practicing law, so they are hard to keep in a firm because they are more valuable. Hopefully one day you will be in that position.

They find business and create it for themselves, the firm, and/or other people. Finders provide the work so that they and others can bill. They are the most valuable players for firms because without them there is no business, no money, and no employees. This does not mean you can ignore being a Minder or a Grinder entirely as you need to do good work and keep clients.

To put it in perspective, if you were the employer, who would you hire as an attorney? The smart guy who has no business, the hard worker who has no business, or the attorney who brings in the business? The answer every time is the attorney who brings the business. Why? Because you need him or her before you focus on the actual practicing of law. On an additional positive note, Grinders generally have business sense that helps them practice some aspects of law better, as that is also part of the analysis to be employed on each matter.

If you take the following advice in the book, hopefully you will become a Finder, a business generator who creates business for yourself and your firm, which in turn makes you an extremely valuable commodity. The best part is that it is not too hard to accomplish.

Chapter Two

General Ideas for Understanding Business Generation

It's important to understand *why* people choose someone as an attorney. There are so many factors to consider, but in the end, there are only certain general concepts that govern business generation and how it works.

For instance, to get business, you need to know people and meet people. (Really not that hard to understand.)

Next, people want to do business with people they like or with whom they connect. There is not much of a difference in ability between attorneys in any industry, so how come some people flock to some attorneys for business and other attorneys cannot generate a nickel of business?

For starters, people will flock to you if they connect with you or even simply because they like you. How often do you call people you do not like for business? Ever have a bad experience at a great store or restaurant? If so, you probably didn't go back.

CONNECTIONS

You need a connection with someone to get their business or referral. People do business with people they like and trust. Let's review connections with potential clients and referral sources.

1. New clients. Connections are important to people who are looking to hire an attorney. That is the main reason they will hire one over the rest. A client walks in and talks about their matter and how they need help. They do not just want any attorney, they want someone who truly understands and connects with their problem. Put yourself in their shoes. They want someone who sees eye to eye with them. Without a connection of any sort, you are not getting hired. I do not care if you are in the law review, the valedictorian of your class, or the smartest person in the world. You need a connection before you are chosen.

If you are a person who understands a client's predicament and connects with your client, they will go home and talk to their spouse about your connection (they will also talk about the case). The main point is that if they proceed, they will choose you because of your connection. At the end of the day, attorneys are simply glorified salesmen selling our services to a consumer. The only way to effectuate that deal is by first standing in the shoes of the consumer in order to truly understand what they are thinking and ultimately connect with them and close a sale of your services.

Not every case is a slam dunk or an easy matter, and you will find yourself recognizing that more and more often. You need to not make it about the client as much as you make it about the case. You must understand that you are not promising or guaranteeing anything to the client about the outcome of the case, you are simply empathizing with them. Additionally, do not forget that principle drives clients. Who better to represent them than an attorney who shares the same principles?

For example, in a scenario where a client has a bad case that has just been presented, a possible—and effective—response might be, "I feel terrible for what you are going through. I cannot believe the other people are being so despicable, but the law is not quite on your side as much as I would like it to be. I believe you might get a sympathy vote from a judge or jury, if that helps, because naturally, nobody could ever like the other side. But we do have a battle. In fact, it will be a tough case."

Guess what? The moment clients connect with attorneys who make them feel as if they understand and share their feelings, the clients feel comfortable with the attorneys. Clients seek empathy in an attorney more than anything, and it is one of the most overlooked qualities in attorneys. You should feel bad for your clients—they need help.

The point of my rambling is that every matter is *personal* to the client, and what they want to hear is that you are with them and that you understand their experience and how bad it has been. They want the connection with you. (On a sidenote, let the client talk about themselves—the more you know, the more opportunities you will find to connect.) Always excel and master the art of listening. Few do.

If a client connects with you or likes you, you will be hired. From now on, remember that the client will hire the attorney they connect with, so listen and see if you can relate to them. If you can accomplish this, your conversion of potential clients will be over 95 percent.

Once you connect, you will begin to convert more business than someone with the highest score on the bar exam or someone who reminds the client of how weak their cases are. In addition, your reputation will grow, which leads to more referrals.

2. Referral sources. The next type of connection to focus on is the new referral source. The same rules apply. If you both have the same philosophies, work ethic, or common ground (e.g., both of you golf), then you become the focus of referrals from the referral source. Getting business is always about connections. When you sit down with someone for the first time as a referral source, listen to them. Let them talk.

People like to talk about themselves (including me, as evidenced by this book), so if you focus and become a person interested in *their* story, they will like you. There is no need to talk right away, they know what you do. Let them feel good about themselves. Once you understand their personal information and their business, it is time to respond. You are never to start with your focus on *your* business—try to find the connection you have with them by listening.

Listen to them. Let them talk. Discover the connection, whether it college, high school, sports, children, books, friends, or even Facebook. It is very rare that you can sit with someone for an hour or meet someone and not have something in common with them.

You want other people to do the talking. At the end, tie it in and make a brief pitch, and that is all. You should try practicing an explanation of what you do and who can send you business in under forty-five seconds, but it should always be kept light, unscripted, and brief (e.g., "By the way, just keep me in mind for some referrals, including real estate, sales, leases, and bank deals. I get most of my business from real estate agents and lenders. If you know anyone, I would love to meet them.") Keep your speech short and sweet. The less you talk and the more you listen, the more business will come to you.

For instance, a few months ago, I had lunch with a financial advisor. He told me his story and we discussed how unique his practice was. Interestingly, he wants to expand, but does not trust people to work with his clients. Rather than talking shop, we talked about the issues in the market. It was a real conversation. He then told me about people he was speaking to about possibly coming aboard. It turned out that I knew one of them (I actually went to camp with him). We spoke about our mutual friend for fifteen minutes. Then he told me about his networking groups. I identified a few friends in one of the groups. We were wrapping up lunch and I had not even talked about myself. He then started asking me about my practice. The point is, now that I know him somewhat, and know we have a connection, I am at the top of his list. You have to connect or get along with someone in order to earn their business. Nobody cares when you tell them how great an attorney you are. I've met many professionals with academic pedigrees or outstanding reputations, but if they are arrogant, offensive, or do not understand or value a referral relationship, that will be our last meeting.

I always find it amazing when a new person asks how can I become *their client* in the first two minutes. With no connection at all, as I stated above, there is no business. Try to find the bond that will have the referral source thinking you are unique and better suited to work with their clients. If I have no connection with them, I will never refer them business. Referral source connections are an important factor in generating business. Focus on any connections with people as you will be remembered for them, and this will create more business.

Hopefully you now have a better understanding of the need to connect.

THE IMPORTANCE OF ATTITUDE AND DELIVERY

People hire positive, confident, and aggressive attorneys more often than those with opposite traits. Once you exude these qualities, clients will migrate to you and you will develop more business. They want that type of person advocating for them, and they do not want to hear the negative when selecting a new attorney (the same goes for existing clients). They want someone who they feel can get the job done.

Presuming you have analyzed the case and it is time to talk with a potential client about their case, your first method of response could either be "Your case is uphill and there is very little chance at winning" or be "The other side will do all the following in response to our approach."

Alternate methods of response are as follows:

A. "Hey there, your case sucks, but there is a chance I can win it. And guess what? I will do my best. I feel bad for you, and all that matters is whether a judge or jury will share the same sentiments . . ."
B. "Let me tell you what I like about your case . . ."
C. "Let me tell you some of the hiccups . . ."
D. "In the end, this will be our focus . . ."
E. "I do not guarantee anything except that I will do my best for you."

The delivery of what I call "ear candy" for the client is the only way to connect with them. They are hearing what they want on the positive side.

Do not forget, they are also hearing the negative, but if they are going to proceed, they may go with you because of the *positive delivery*. Which attorney would you choose? Both say the same thing, but the alternate methods of response are positive. The alternate methods of response will be selected every single time. Do not forget—you are there to advocate and be a representative for the client—do you really think a Debbie Downer attitude is what they want? Being positive is the *most* important aspect of landing a client when providing analysis.

As I mentioned earlier, I truly never understand the entirely negative approach. As attorneys, we can never guarantee and must always advise of the risks. Why then, if the case is so bad, do you guarantee you are going to lose? As long as you advise the client of the risks, you are fine. There are just two different approaches to doing it, and although the case may not be winnable, at least you are giving it a shot with a positive approach.

Remember, positive attorneys are the ones who get hired. Just like coaching, if the coach *only* tells the players that they will lose, the players believe it. If the coach can recognize strengths, the players will be more inspired. Using our analogy, you should be that coach.

The last bit of delivery that does not work for everyone, but should always be considered is the "bulldog delivery." Do not just be positive, be aggressive. Truthfully, I do take clients' matters personally and I can lose my temper, so most of the advice in this book is based on my instincts (in fact, the only thing I have to think about is *not* getting too worked up and *not* yelling). Being aggressive is, in fact, natural for me.

One thing is definite: nobody wants the sissy lawyer. Everyone wants the bulldog. Clients want a tough attorney—that is why they hire attorneys. You do not necessarily have to want the fight if it can be avoided, but you are *not afraid* of the fight, or anything else for that matter.

Remember: if aggressiveness is not a natural trait of yours, try to make it one. Take the matter personally, put yourself in the client's shoes, and try to feel like they do.

One attorney I worked with in the past was notoriously methodical to his detriment. Clients would always complain

4L – THE CLASS NEVER TAUGHT IN LAW SCHOOL | 97

that he had no fight in him (the irony was that he was a litigation attorney and I am primarily transactional). I used to remind him to not be too smart, to not be too lawyerlike for the client. They want someone who will take the gloves off and fight.

Then one day, he was dealing with an unethical attorney (imagine that), and he came down and told me about the terrible time he was having. He said he was going to get *her* at all costs. (He also indicated that the client hated the other attorney to the point where they both connected in that mutual feeling.) I reminded him of the message I relay to all my clients about the battle that I will wage for them. I also reminded him how strong his connection was with this client. Plain and simple, you cannot change your personality for people, but you can move a little if it creates a better connection with the client and gets you the business. Furthermore, now when I give the attorney above a new matter, I remind him what the client really wants, and that puts him in more of a game mode. His results and connections with clients have been outstanding ever since and now they look to him on new matters.

Next point - be authoritative. When you visit a doctor, nobody likes the back and forth. You want the doctor to tell you what to do. It is the same concept with lawyers. Tell the client the approach in the end rather than bouncing back and forth with no direction simply because you are nervous

Next, nobody wants a wimp representing them. (Do I really have to waste ink and say this?)

As for existing clients, you must maintain a positive attitude. If every conversation includes you beating them down with bad news or a negative outlook, they will feel that you are not right for their case, and I would think they are right. Also, clients do not want to hear your Cover Your Ass (CYA) speech every day. I cannot tell you how many times I hear a new client tell me that all their last attorney did was tell them how negative their case was—they forgot to say anything positive.

Existing clients are sensitive, and should never feel like the underappreciated friend. Like certain friends who need to hear they look good, clients need to hear *good* things to make them feel at ease. Nobody leaves you if they hear the positive points of their case, even if they are not strong positions.

In summary, your attitude and delivery to the client are very important aspects of not only keeping clients, but generating new business. Additionally, try to be the bulldog and people will choose you over other "weak" and "negative" attorneys for their cases, even if it is a weak case and they know it.

WHO BECOMES A CLIENT?

You need clients for business, so how do you find them?

First, there are clients who come into your office through referrals, et al. That is pretty easy. But in addition to that, every person you meet knows or is a potential client for you, directly or indirectly. Everyone has the potential to be a client, whether now or in the future, or alternatively, they could refer a new client. People are very shortsighted. They only look at the now, whether a person can be a client today. If not, they are not interested in that person. This is a terrible approach because that person could be a client down the road.

The real lost opportunity, though, is that the people who are not clients right now know potential clients, whether now or in the future. Everyone knows at least ten thousand people, and if you meet one, they have the ability to refer one or more of their ten thousand to you. Not everyone has to send you business. All they have to do is introduce you to someone else who may send you business. This is called the *indirect referral*, and has benefited both me personally and my firm in the nature of new business. Lawyers are very simple and shortsighted in that all they see is one level—can this person send me business or be a client? If not, they move on. Do not stop there. Meet people and invite their referrals. Meet as many people as you can and ask them for introductions to other *good* people. Direct referrals are great, but they are not always attainable. Remember, any introduction or indirect referral is a good introduction because every person is either a potential client or knows a potential client. Indirect referrals are always a possibility, and you need to always be aware of and open to them.

If you know a lot of people, the indirect referrals are the easiest way for people to connect, and they often turn into direct referrals.

If you do not meet at least one person a day (including weekends), your day is lost. I do not care if that person will never use you. If you meet them and connect, they can and will introduce you to their personal list of good people, which will turn into business for you. When I go to the airport, I realize there are so many people I do not represent. The point is that there are many business opportunities out there, and the only way to get them is to know everyone, or at least as many people as possible. The more people you know, the better off you will be for referrals.

A NEW APPROACH TO REFERRALS

Recognize that every person is a potential client, but what do you do next to get business? Now it is time to take an entirely different approach for getting referrals. It is time to focus on *giving* referrals. The more business you give, the more you get.

It's time to focus on the direct and indirect referrals for others, because as you provide them, so you will receive in return. You need to introduce people to other people for business and referrals, direct or indirect, so they will all benefit.

Always think of how other people get their business and who their clients are, and introduce them to the appropriate people. Put them together with other people who can help or might need their services, or even put a group of people together so they can exchange business opportunities.

Think about the indirect referral and how easy it is to give. As I said, everyone knows ten thousand people. An accountant, for example, gets business from real estate agents. I know about thirty accountants, so I put an accountant and a real estate agent together. That is my referral. They may not work on each other's business, but if they cross paths with a number of people, it is more than likely that business will be exchanged between them in some way. For example, the real estate agent could know someone in need of an accountant. Guess what? They refer.

What happens next? Hopefully they will try to send me business, as I have helped both of them, and most successful people try to give *back* when they receive. Apply this approach with everyone.

Some real estate agents ask me if I know anyone buying or selling. By the time I do, they usually have an agent at that point. But, I do know lenders who need business from real estate agents, and they also know potential buyers and sellers, so I put them together.

Do not be shortsighted. You should spend every spare minute attempting to put people together or trying to meet new people who you can introduce to your contacts. Every time I have lunch with someone, I am having lunch with everyone they know and vice versa. Let's get those people together to generate more business.

When attempting to make an indirect referral, remember that you should not simply try to bring together people in the same field (e.g., builders and subcontractors). You should bring good people together. If they like each other and/or connect, they will find a way to exchange business, and they will be thankful to you. The worst-case scenario is that no business referral results from the meeting, but you will still have developed a better connection with that person. Plus, you are trying, which is more than most.

People in industries with clients (e.g., accountants) know a lot of people, so you will be surprised at the referrals that get exchanged. The other day I introduced a real estate agent to a financial advisor. I explained that there was not going to be any direct business referred, but rather indirect business through their thousands of contacts (they each know more than ten thousand people); they had already started to set up introductions. Be the person who sets up introductions and good things will come.

The joke (because few people actually do this) is that setting up referrals is easy. All you are doing is introducing people to each other. The other day, I introduced a marketing director of a personal-injury firm to a marketing director of an accounting firm. The meeting resulted in very few direct referrals, if any. It turns out they had mutual referral sources, prospects, and friends, so they were working together. Now I get credit for those indirect referrals (and I will continually remind them). It does not really matter because they subscribe to a typical human trait: if someone sends me business, I want to return the favor. Most good people try to send business if they get it. The two of them are now looking out for me, and they are both benefitting from the introduction, which is a win for everyone.

In summary, stop thinking about yourself and take a look at the big picture.

You have the opportunity to send every person you know a referral, whether direct or indirect. Make those introductions. Set up meetings. You will be surprised how much more business you're able to help generate for others, and in return, for you.

You should now always think about helping others and referring business, and you can expect business in return.

Chapter Three

Places to Develop Connections and Meet People

There are so many opportunities to focus on the basic principles/ideas of Chapter Two to generate business. Let's review some of these venues and how you can utilize them for your benefit.

NETWORKING EVENTS

What better way to connect with people, meet new people, and/or to introduce others than to go out with them? There are many events that you can attend to meet people, connect with people, and introduce people to others.

However, this is not simply grabbing lunch, and then hoping you'll hear from them again. You must follow up. Follow up. Follow through. Let's go through some different events, and further strategies to be employed so you are making the most out of every meal, event, or occasion in which you are participating.

1. Meals and drinks. Eating three meals a day and having drinks at night gives you twenty-eight opportunities to make new contacts every week. Throw in early afternoon coffee and you are up to thirty-five opportunities. Nobody can do thirty-five, but you should shoot for seven to ten. Every time you go out, you can meet ten thousand potential new referrals, and all you have to do is connect with *one* person.

For starters, pick a few restaurants that are popular and eat there regularly. After some time, you will start to recognize people and they will recognize you. I might say, "I always see you here. I am Greg R. Cohen . . ." Then hand them a card. (I do not give out my cards anymore, as once I receive someone's card, the ball is in my court and I can then reach out to them, as set forth below). A new introduction can come simply from recognizing someone. Follow up with an e-mail. Next time, there will be more interaction. And next time, there will be a new client or referrals. Remember, everyone knows at least ten thousand people. When you see your new contact the next time, introduce *them* to anyone you just met with and both people will be appreciative. Plus, for the new person you are meeting for breakfast, you are already trying to give them business. It's a nice way to start a relationship.

Another benefit to eating at only a few places is that when everyone knows you and says hello, you look important to other people. If you look important to other people, then you appear to be someone everybody will want to know. Have you ever watched somebody walk through a room and shake hands with everyone? You want to meet that person. You can become that person by picking a new bar to frequent in an up-scale area. In total, fifteen guys go once a week for six weeks. Guess what? We are all meeting each of the fifteen for referrals, and now we are getting to know more of the regulars who frequent that restaurant. It's that simple. All you have to do is meet one new person every time you go out and try to introduce them to someone else.

The strategic meal is also a great way to catch up, not only with the person you are with, but with everyone you see and run into that day. How often do you see friends, clients, or potential clients when out to eat? It usually creates a good opportunity to follow up with them afterward. People do not constantly think about lawyers, so every reminder or follow-up puts you at the top of their list, sort of like Google. Be fresh in their minds. (We will discuss follow-up later and how it can be used effectively for this very purpose.)

At the meal, do not forget to make it about the other person, not about you. Let them talk about themselves. Listen. Always lay low. Your time will come. Find connections. Breakfasts and lunches are like busy speed dating events for everyone, so you only have a little time to connect and make an impression (utilize the forty-five-second routine that we discussed earlier).

I also try to strategize with whomever I am meeting about who they are looking for as a client. Every time I am done, I think of at least one person I can introduce them to afterward. When I return to the office, I immediately send an e-mail introducing both to each other. Now a potential referral is made, and I get the credit. It is important to do this immediately after the meal, or you will forget. A missed introduction is a lost opportunity.

Dinners and/or drinks are always the best means of getting to know a person, connecting on the highest level, and making them a client or referral source. Everyone can have a boring breakfast, but dinners and drinks are socially driven. If you have a drink with someone on a good night out and you connect, it will lead to business for both parties. I find that everyone who has ever had a drink with someone has connected with that other person in some form or fashion.

Lastly, the same rules apply to frequenting the same bar after hours. The bar scene allows people to come up to you and facilitates introductions.

Be the person who is always out and always introducing others.

2. Law functions. Go to law functions, and not just the good ones. Try the criminal lawyers' happy hour even if you are not a criminal attorney. Meet people *outside* of your area of practice. They can send you the most business, as they may not know many attorneys in your field. You can also send them business. In this way, you are building a database, so if a client calls you for any other matter, you have a referral for them.

Also, if you get involved with your bar association, more people will recognize you. You will also meet your opposition and the judges. The better your dealings are with your peers, the easier your life will be.

3. Networking groups. Breakfast networking groups are good for meeting people. Getting together with twenty to thirty people every week or every other week would be tough otherwise. Now you are fresh in their minds. Plus, you only miss half an hour of billable time because you are in around 9:00 a.m. or 9:30 a.m. (You can also call and bill on the way in, so it's not a total loss).

Lunch networking events are tough because they eat up so much time during the day that you cannot get to your work. Nonetheless, the mood is usually better because not everyone is irritated about getting up so early. Weekly networking groups have a type of cult or fraternity feel, but it is very good because people have to continually provide referrals, and, if nothing else, at least got to meet thirty-five to fifty people who you can introduce to others for referrals.

I recently joined the Inns of Court—a "legal fraternity," as I refer to it. First, you meet new lawyers in the area. Even if you do not get a great deal of referral business, it is a good way to meet people. Regardless, if you meet three hundred new lawyers, you will get more business directly or indirectly than you would have had you never met them - that is guaranteed. Plus, you can always find people who are in a certain area of law that you now can refer to, so your database is getting full.

For litigators, among others, there are also a lot of judges that join the group, so you get to meet them on a personal basis. You may also learn the good and bad about practicing litigation in a courtroom from a judge's standpoint, as well as from experienced litigation attorneys. Any time you can attend an event at which you learn something, you are bettering yourself as an attorney.

Back to networking and marketing yourself to others. One new referral source can equate to major money for you and/or your referrals, so do not miss any of these opportunities.

I was recently speaking to a friend of mine and I mentioned the Inns. He told me he had no interest because he was in-house counsel and there was *no benefit* to him. He was so wrong. You must get the big picture. Regardless of your current position, if you are getting business today, you may need those contacts down the road. Every night out and every meeting counts. The more people you know, the more people there are who can refer business to you and vice versa.

Join other large networking groups, such as business development boards and attorney accountant groups, among others. All these groups provide you with opportunities to meet at least one new person per meeting. It adds up. Build your network through all means possible. That is how it is done. The more direct and indirect referrals you have to give, the more you will receive.

4. Happy hours. I organize a happy hour every two weeks and invite ten to twenty people of different professions. Those introductions are my referrals (also, keep tabs of the introductions so you can follow up with everyone to remind them of those referrals). Find an attorney who does not do your type of work. Follow up with them. Invite them to one of your happy hours and introduce them to others. Understanding this is a new level of networking—indirect business generates new business, and new meetings. Now you have potentially referred some business to twenty other people, and you will get it back.

I have a friend who sets up a quarterly happy hour for four hundred people (85 percent of the attendees are attorneys). You should go to these events and get out there. Meet everyone in attendance and then meet every person they know.

You also need to find the different approaches to meet more people. I went to one of the events, and out of the forty people I knew, five asked if I knew a person across the room and that person happened to be a friend of mine. For the next meeting of that happy hour, I called my friend ahead of time and told him I wanted him to come to our designated area for at least thirty minutes in the hopes that I could introduce him to everyone who came up. Suddenly, I was working for him *and* my friends.

By the way, at that next event, I introduced him to a number of new people, and he introduced me to new people, as well. At the end of the night, I had introduced him to no fewer than twenty people and he had done the same for me.

The next day, I sent him an e-mail with the contact information for the people I had introduced him to, as he did not have all their cards. I asked him for the same. Everyone benefitted: my original friends, my friend who came over, and me.

The point is, try to find good ideas/approaches on how it is best for you to meet people, put other people together, and send business to others. You should always be trying and working for others and benefits will occur.

5. Steak dinner night. Get together with five strong people who can afford a steak dinner once a quarter and have each person invite five people to attend, so you have a solid group of twenty-five to thirty. This is yet another opportunity to get together and meet new people and connect. You can also do more than one. The more you are out, the more people you will meet and get to know, and the more you will be on their minds.

I am presently invited to three monthly dinners. Within these groups alone, I can introduce members and outside people. As I make more introductions, more business will follow.

6. Other fun events. The best way to get a new client is to get to know them (I believe I have reiterated this at least fifteen times). Do not forget to get together socially. Two to four hours of social time is better than five lunches. You become a person. Play tennis or go boating. Try to get larger groups together to play golf. For instance, I organized a golf "tournement" for twelve people. Everyone bet a little money. When we were done, we had drinks for an hour. You could see the relationships developing, and I was responsible for them. I will happily take credit for these new relationships and remind everyone of my role. What goes around comes around. And on the positive side, you get to have fun.

7. Seminars/public speaking. Try to speak publicly to as many groups as you can. I speak to real estate agents and lenders, but I also branch out of my element. I have been trying to speak to criminal law groups, as they do not overlap much with my field and I would like to be their go-to person. (You need to have a relevant topic, though, which is the hard part.)

You can and *should* bring in backup—lunch. Free lunch makes any speaker more interesting, even me. You can also bring in other speakers and give away a prize by collecting business cards. Now you just picked up fifty new e-mails to follow up with the next day. More people in your database. More people to introduce.

As a reminder for the presentations, people's attention spans are short and sweet. Identify the recipient and get to the point fast.

8. Religious events. Same thing. Get involved. Lots of people attend these events. I play softball on Sunday mornings with twenty guys who take their kids to Sunday school. That's twenty more people and it is fun. What else would you do during this time, watch TV? Eat Twinkies?

9. Sports leagues. Golf leagues, tennis leagues, softball leagues, shooting clubs. You get to have fun and meet new people.

10. Charities. Find some you like, but look for your demographic. In Palm Beach County, I prefer the Happy Camper Foundation, Jupiter Police Foundation and local Palm Beach Gardens Youth Athletic Association. Their events are often social and fun, and include a number of people. If you decide to attend a charity event, get there early because you will only have one hour to say hello to as many people as possible. Try to meet at least a few new people, and if you know someone, focus on introducing others. Plus, it is for a good cause.

11. Football and college events. When I moved back to Palm Beach Gardens, I knew four Pittsburgh Steelers fans, all with the same last name. I met other fans at the "Steelers bars," and guess what? I found some Steelers business. Plus, you have a great connection. The same goes for college alumni events—you need to go and meet people. There are people to meet at every outing. Go Canes!

SUMMARY

Attending any event helps you meet people and connect with people, and/or provides opportunities to create business for others and yourself. Every missed opportunity is money lost for you, so get out and get involved.

You need to do everything possible to brand yourself and grow your name and reputation. Anyone can practice law, but having a book of business makes you a commodity. Always bring cards with you, hand them out, and get others' cards in return. With every person you meet, you should attempt to either get together at a later time or introduce them to another person. Those are referrals and you will get them back. Do not be shortsighted and focus on yourself. When you focus on *giving*, the *getting* will come.

Chapter Four

Follow-Up

If only creating a loyal, lifelong client was as easy as having lunch or talking on the phone. It doesn't happen like that. You need to constantly follow up with every person you meet; you should be the person on their mind, otherwise you have lost an opportunity.

GENERAL FOLLOW-UP

You have now realized that business does not fall in your lap, and that you have to go out and find it by meeting new people. That is the first part. The second part is ensuring you are being thought of and have been remembered. In order to achieve that goal, you must always follow up on everything.

If you are fresh in somebody's mind, they will remember you and potentially send business your way. Follow up *every minute that you can*. Make people remember you.

After every meeting, meal, and encounter, follow up with an e-mail or phone call.

If you think of someone, follow up by saying, "I have not talked to you lately. How is everything?"

As previously mentioned I always carry a Dictaphone or a pen. When I see someone, I make a note to follow up with them.

Did you meet a few lawyers at a bar function? Send them each an e-mail saying, "It was nice to meet you." Weekend follow-ups are good, as well; if you are friendly, it will be a good time to learn what is going on.

Connections always stay firm if you continually follow up.

Following up also serves as an advertisement and/or reminder of who you are. If you are fresh in people's minds, they will think of you first for business.

You should follow up even if you are being brushed off by a client. Some people/clients think and hope matters will work themselves out so they may not call back after the initial discussion. It is up to you to continually follow up and ensure that the matter has worked itself out or at least that you will be the person representing them, as you have gone above and beyond what anyone else would do. People are shocked when I call them to follow up after our first discussions. They are surprised to hear from an attorney who follows up because they are used to attorneys who are primarily reactive. I am now fresh in their minds and I will be remembered.

Following up on new potential clients is often missed, costing you and your firm a tremendous amount of money. It is very rare that an attorney initiates the follow-up; most simply wait for the client to call them. This is a terrible approach.

Let's look at a basic example of how a simple follow-up with a potential client can help you generate business:

The client or potential client calls with a question, problem, or need, or a referral source sends someone your way. Whatever it is, you address their request with a quick "free" discussion. By now, you should have already sent a thank-you note to the referral source (never forget this). A few days go by and you have heard nothing. You need to follow up with your client or potential client. (By the way, this is so simple, it is a must.)

Naturally, the phone is the most personal way to communicate, but it is not necessary at this stage. All it takes is an e-mail to your contact, such as "Anything happening regarding the matter we discussed?" If you have less time, you can simply say, "Any word?" The results will be incredible. If they respond no, remind them you are waiting and tell them, "Okay, let me know." What if they say yes? You now can ask, "What happened?" The best part about this scenario is that it takes three seconds, and it is the client that must do the explaining in his or her e-mail. Now, when you're done reading, call the client to remind them what you can do for them. A positive result always needs the final follow-up.

Let's analyze what just happened. You gave your typical five to ten minutes of free advice, and not only are you on the client's mind, but you were the one who initiated it. You did not have to wait for them to call you. Be proactive so your clients will recognize that you are thinking about them, rather than waiting for them to think about you. Every client will appreciate you making the effort to reach out, as it makes them feel important. On top of it, you now have the inroads to remind the client about your practice. Following up with the potential client is not waiting for them to call. Make the call yourself and be remembered.

Here's a quick tip for those of you who are not quite as organized: whenever you do something—communicate with a client, provide initial assistance, or make a phone call—prepare an e-mail in your drafts immediately after to go out a few days later as a follow-up. Every Friday or Monday, send those e-mails out. You will probably forget to follow up with everyone, which is why I recommend preparing the follow-up e-mail immediately after the first contact. You should always remember to prepare that draft, as following up goes a long way in the minds of the clients.

Here are two other examples of how the follow-up e-mail can be used:

A. After any meal, I follow up with an e-mail saying, "Good to meet you." Next, I create and save another draft as a second follow-up or make a note on my calendar to send another e-mail, which should be done in two months.

B. After every lunch, as I indicated earlier, I not only make the introductions, but I also prepare a follow-up asking, "Anything happen with _____? I previously sent you their information." I usually send this e-mail about two weeks later. Now you are on their mind again and trying to get them business.

Do not forget about unsolicited follow-ups. I think every day I have an opportunity to follow up with at least five people I know, but have not been in touch with lately. An average attorney might ask, "Why would I waste my time doing that?" Again, sending a relevant note or reminder simply asking how someone is doing places you at the forefront of their mind. When you are in someone's mind, they remember you! The more you remind them, the better the chance they will refer you for business or refer you to someone else.

IDEAS FOR FOLLOW-UP

Follow-up is not merely a reaction to a meal or event. You can create it yourself and/or find it in other places. Opportunities to follow up are everywhere.

For example, I read two newspapers (old school – I know) every morning. Every time I see something positive (e.g., an article, a write-up, or an award) about someone I know, I tear it out and send it to them as soon as I get to the office. Is that a terrible idea and a waste of time? Of course not. By reaching out to someone I know, I am showing them I care. Have any of you ever been in the paper? Obviously, when someone takes the time to call or e-mail, you are thankful for that effort. You also tell others that he or she reached out to you. The point is, by doing something simple and thoughtful, you are creating a discussion about yourself and reminding people that you exist.

If you want to follow up further with that person for their recognition, I recommend organizing a get-together or a phone call (if you do talk on the phone, make sure you only talk about them). Do not sell yourself, as the phone call is meant to celebrate *their accomplishment*. If you meet in person, there will be enough time to tell them how great you are.

I speak to a certain client on a regular basis and she is always in the paper. One morning not long ago, I saw her mentioned. I guess I was feeling lazy, because I did not cut out the picture and send it to her. When I spoke to her about her matter a few days later, I told her about the picture and how I didn't send it to her because she was in the paper so much and probably sick of getting my e-mails. It turns out she had not seen the picture. The first thing I did when I got home was locate the paper (in the recycling bin) and I sent it to her the next day with a note. All of a sudden, I became the attorney who went out of his way for a client just to send them a clipping. Clients appreciate effort and caring. Simple acts like this will distinguish you from other attorneys, remind people about you, and lead to more business. Always be on people's minds. Follow-up accomplishes this.

I also send articles to people that they may find interesting. Who knows what may come of it? The point is, only good can come from it for your client or contact and you are now on their mind. Plus, they might enjoy the article!

1. Look for and think about new clients after reading an article or watching the news. I saw a new company was coming to the area, so I told a client about it because they could potentially get business from that company. The news offers many opportunities for follow-up.

2. Pull up the local lawsuits. See if a client or person you know is getting sued. Reach out to them. They may have forgotten you, but now you are back. If you are qualified, call the attorney and perhaps serve as an expert witness. If the case is similar to one you've handled in the past, call and offer some advice (but make sure you wait until the pending matter is over to avoid a conflict of interest).

3. Whenever you see someone, always remind yourself to follow up with them. All you need is a simple e-mail saying, "Good to see you today. Hope all is well." Again, now you have reminded the client or potential client about you and you'll be on their mind.

4. When you attend an event, make sure you get people's cards. I also bring a pen so I can write a thing or two about the person on the card as a reminder (e.g., "Very ugly little guy who looks like Larry from *The Three Stooges*"). This will help you recall the conversation even better when you are following up the next day. (In that case, as part of my free advice, probably best not to mention the ugly look.) For example, you might say, "It was good to meet you. I enjoyed talking about _____."

5. Send holiday cards. When the cards are personal, clients remember you. Sign them yourself and write individual notes. I actually sat at a function with one guy who sends me a holiday card every year, but he did not know who I was. What a joke!

Write something on the card in *your own handwriting*, not just your preprinted signature.

6. Use social media. Facebook, LinkedIn, and Twitter are always good places to find information for follow-ups. Read people's updates. You never know when someone may have a matter that you can now follow up on. Anything—a lawsuit, a new baby, a death, a house. Everyone makes announcements. You are just following up.

7. Use events and sports to your advantage. If you know someone is a fan, congratulate them on their team's big win. Do not follow up if they lose. No one wants to hear "Sorry you did not win." It may sound sincere, but it is irritating.

8. Follow up with everyone on every deal after transactions have closed. "Congratulations." "How did we do?" "How do you get your clients?" You stand out from the other 90 percent because you are an attorney who actually follows up. This is the reason people like us and will refer business to us. You are also now meeting new people who you can introduce to others.

If you are exhausted at this stage, that is a good sign—now you are getting it! Just wait, it is not that hard. The interesting transition will be when you get ninety-nine clients and lose one because you did not follow up. You will be upset at yourself because you did not correct the one issue, which feels a lot like losing a wallet full of cash.

SUMMARY

Send those follow-up emails (by the way, any e-mails above should come from your professional e-mail address with all your details listed). Be on people's minds. Make them think about you.

Follow-up is integral to maintaining relationships with people. No matter what you do or how hard you work, without client follow-up, your results will be lost, and without follow-up to the other parties, you are losing business. You will be surprised how often a person has a new matter for you when you follow up. The goal is to be on people's minds when an issue arises, and nobody out there is doing this except me.

Chapter Five

Refreshers and Bits and Pieces

I have spent more than twenty years building my practice. For the last twenty-four months, I have taken notes on the things I do every day and included them in this book. Whether they are different from what everyone else does, I do not know. I do know these tips work. Follow at least one and you will generate more business. Follow all and you will be a machine.

1. Make sure your e-mail signature contains all your information, including firm name and phone number, and cell phone number. The question is, do you put your specialty in your e-mail signature? It could limit business if your firm brings in other work, but it will be visible. Generally, if you are involved in a more social e-mail exchange with banter going back and forth, and you do not know most of the people, I would add your area of focus. It is easy for others to see and might stick in their minds. (My signature includes "Real Estate.") Recently, I found myself in the same situation above, and out of the ninety-plus people on the list, two called me right away. Do you ever read people's e-mail signatures? Of course. So do others.

2. Get board certified. I took the test and clients know. I can tell everyone that I am an expert. This information is included in my e-mail signature. Every person sees "Real Estate" and "Expert" in my e-mail *every time*. It makes a lasting impression.

3. Become an officer or director of law groups/committees of the local bar association. It looks good on paper, sounds good to the masses, and allows you to get involved with officers and directors of the other groups who do not practice your type of law, resulting in more referrals back and forth.

4. Create a mass database. Save any general mass e-mails and add those people to your own list. I have a list of thousands of people and I use it when I make a firm announcement.

5. Look through any list e-mails from others and see if there is any business or person you want to meet. If so, have the person who sent you the e-mail make an introduction. For example, every company that assists my clients on due diligence when they are buying property has been introduced to me in this way.

6. When you add to your contacts list, it is always good to include the name, the place of employment, and the *job description* in the title so it is easiest to locate. For example,

I searched soil tests the other day and two companies came up. You cannot remember everyone.

7. Keep a database of people you introduce. This is something I always do. If I see them, I can pull it up and ask them if there was business. I can also remind them I made the introduction.

8. Do not be complacent or take the client for granted. Always be thankful for the clients. If you appreciate the relationship, you will have a closer bond, you will be a better attorney, and you will generate and maintain more business. When you lose one client, you lose money.

9. Use every minute. Learn to wake up early, or as I say, "Do not sleep your life away." Get an extra hour or two in the morning for billing et al. This leaves more time for networking, marketing, and everything else. When your eyes pop open at 5:00 a.m., get out of bed. Do not try to go back to sleep. Every minute available should be used to practice or generate. When you're done, enjoy your time socially. (Combining generating and socializing is the ultimate goal.) When you go to the bathroom, read an e-mail or send a follow-up. When you walk to your car, make the follow-up phone call. And how often are you driving twenty minutes in the morning somewhere with nothing to do? Use that time to your benefit and make phone calls.

10. Say happy birthday. I'm not a huge fan of following up with people on birthdays by e-mail. If you want to wish someone a happy birthday, make sure you *call* them. E-mails are not personal enough.

11. Remember those holiday cards. As I said, handwrite something personal to each person (e.g., "I look forward to seeing you!"). At least hint that you care. The corporate card is *not* enough.

12. Make yourself available on weekends for clients; at a minimum, call new clients on the weekends. *New* clients who do not know you will see that you are a hard worker who cares about your clients. Taking the time to call a new client on the weekend is very important to that person. Everyone else can wait until Monday.

13. Ask for business. Do not be shy. When the time comes, you will know. You need to put people on the spot. I had a friend who asked me for free legal advice (just a few questions). I reminded him that this is how I support my family, and I am hopeful he appreciates the free work, but maybe he could think about referring paying work. Things have now changed. *If you do not ask, you will not get.*

14. If you hear someone is unhappy with their job, try to find a new place for them. Put them in touch with others and use the same concept described earlier. Helping people is the same as a referral. They will appreciate what you have done for them, and if the job works out, they will really appreciate you and try to help you in return. Plus, you did something good.

15. The best referral relationships are when both people feel like they are getting the better end of the deal. This often goes hand in hand with feeling that a situation is unfair to the other person. In this relationship, both parties will always work harder for each other.

16. Introducing people in the same field as an indirect referral can generate ideas. Now they can discuss similar problems and bounce ideas off one another. Because it was you who made this happen, they will be grateful.

17. Introducing business-development representatives from different companies (even unrelated) are extraordinary referrals. This is an ultimate type of referral. All those people do all day is network. Now you have combined two huge bubbles. You should also try it with people who have similar jobs (e.g., people in human resources from two different companies). Perhaps they will hit it off. Perhaps they can help each other (e.g., brainstorming situations). If they have something in common, the connection will be made and they will remember that it was you who introduced them.

18. If you have other focuses in your firm, do not forget about their work. When I am actively pursuing a new business owner, I remind them that we have an employment attorney who writes employee handbooks. This is a great opportunity to generate business for your firm. From there, hopefully the relationship will grow. Certain clients will associate you with a specialty, so you should always remind them of the other work.

19. Do not forget about the existing clients dealing with other attorneys in your firm. You need to follow up with them so that they do not feel ignored. If someone else in your firm worked on something, follow up. "Glad it worked out. How is everything?" Do not ever be shy about calling because sometimes e-mailing does not get you there.

20. Follow-up is key. Create a follow-up system, and always remember to follow up. As I mentioned earlier, when someone calls you with a question, you should be able to point them in the right direction. Send a follow-up e-mail in a few days. Now you are the attorney who followed up, which is more than most people would do. The same goes for new clients on the phone. Follow up with a potential client even if they do not follow up with you. Sometimes you need that second call to make someone get off the fence. You will be surprised how often I hear "I was just thinking about calling you." When you follow up, they are assured that proceeding with you was the right thing to do.

21. A new matter and follow-up lists are very important. If you get interviewed for a matter, put a summary on that list and follow up over the next few days after the meeting. If you don't receive a call back, keep making the effort.

22. Return every phone call and return it fast. Calls from new clients should be returned within two hours. If you're unavailable, ask your assistant call to let the client know when you will call. Calls from existing clients should be returned in twelve to twenty-four hours. Clients are under the gun and the quicker you call them back, the better off you will be. I cannot tell you how many times an associate has failed to return a call within a few hours and how many times that has resulted in lost business. If you are too busy, *have someone call to say you will call later.* One missed phone call can translate to losses of thousands of dollars and a tarnished reputation (e.g., "He doesn't return calls"). Please remind yourself of this tip.

I make a note of every phone call I receive on a legal pad. I have never missed a call back since I started this habit. (Get rid of those small phone call notes, too. They're too easy to lose.) This is the first thing I ever learned (thank you, Petie).

Fifteen percent of people who are looking for a new attorney are doing so because a previous lawyer never returned their phone calls. When I acquire a new client, the first thing I do is give them my cell phone number. I send an e-mail with it and tell the client to call me anytime. Everyone knows I return phone calls. Everyone knows which attorneys do not return phone calls. One missed call could mean two years of lost rent or mortgage payments.

4L – THE CLASS NEVER TAUGHT IN LAW SCHOOL | 129

23. Referrals come from other attorneys, so always try to maintain those relationships. Attorneys also have conflicts—be their go-to person and vice versa. (Remember: an e-mail lasts forever, so if you are fighting with someone, call them. Do not put it in an e-mail.)

24. Even if a mutual client uses another firm for work, you should still follow up. Ask them if the experience was good. Be the "follow-up king." The attorney who cares the most gets the gig. Plus, you never know when an opportunity will present itself to you or another member of your firm.

25. Focus. Always focus on what makes you a strong attorney when speaking to a new client. I have a friend who advertises being a specialist in certain type of back surgery. I tell people I may not be the oldest or smartest, but everyone knows that nobody fucks with my clients. Clients like to hear the confidence.

Also, if it is appropriate, focus on your accolades. For example, I am part of the Palm Beach County Bar Association's Real Estate Committee and used to be the Chariman. Is that a big deal? No, but to a client it sounds good.

Lastly, focus on yourself and what differentiates you from others. For example, real estate is not the most complicated thing, but I approach it with my own unique perspective.

26. All clients want an aggressive or "bulldog" attorney. People tell me, "I hear you are a bulldog" at least twice a day. Nobody ever called and asked for an attorney and said, "I want a wimp." Exude some strength.

27. Give free advice when asked, but keep it brief. Need to lure the client a little. Also, keep tabs and notes of the free advice you give. You can use it if a client or potential client has abused the relationship by taking and not giving. Now is the time to remind them how you support your family.

When you're done giving free advice, send the follow-up e-mail and always remember to *ask* for good business. People's dependence on you, even if it is for free advice, transfers into real business.

People need to know they can call you and not get a bill. Existing clients want attorneys who will not send them a bill for thirty-five dollars for a brief conversation. You want people to know that if someone has an issue, they can call you to ask if you can handle it.

28. People are sometimes uncomfortable working with their friends. Let your friends know you like being a lawyer, especially when you can help a friend. You need everyone to know that you are the person to call and you'll figure it out or send them on to someone else.

29. At every function and/or meal, try to get at least a minimum of one new contact. Just one.

30. Never be "too busy" or let a client know they come second. Clients should feel like they are your priority. If you're delayed in getting back to them, you should apologize.

Do not *ever* tell people how busy or great your business is. A simple response of "good" or "we are busy" is sufficient when talking about your practice. Words like "slammed" make you sound unprofessional.

You do not want the client to feel unimportant. You are never too busy to work on their matter. Instead, give them a reason such as "I have been out" or "I have been in a closing scheduled for weeks." If you cannot get back to them, have your assistant follow up and give a reason. If you treat a client as second-class, they will find an attorney who treats them like first-class.

31. Use demographics when introducing people or bringing groups together. Consider making introductions by demographics (e.g., younger people, women), as usually *similar* people connect better. Indirect referrals are everywhere.

32. When taking a referral from anyone, especially other lawyers, always speak to the referred person yourself. (This is primarily for personal-injury attorneys.) If you have your in house nurse or doctor call the client in your place, I will not refer to you again. I spend thirty minutes promoting how well I work with the referral source, but if they cannot spend ten minutes on the phone with the client, it will be their last referral from me.

33. Never overstep a referral. If someone sends you a referral, and the potential client needs more work than is within the referring attorney's scope, *send it back.* Do not be *that* person, or your reputation will grow very bad very fast. For example, twelve years ago, I referred a bankruptcy attorney for a matter, and then he gave a small real estate component to someone else in his firm. That was my last referral to him. I also reminded our entire office about his actions, and he received no more referrals from anyone in our firm.

34. Always give any referral source an immediate thank-you for the attempt, and provide updates along the way. If you are referred by someone, always send a follow-up to the source. A basic "Thank you for sending _____ to me" will suffice. People want to hear the updates and be appreciated. I now refuse to send referrals to a few people because they never called or e-mailed me to thank me.

35. After you sign up a client by referral, send another follow-up to the referral source. Hopefully you are always sincere when you receive a referral. If not, you really should take a step back and appreciate any business that is sent to you. Remember, what we do is really not that hard and for someone to trust you to do it for them is really quite remarkable. You should always understand that you are the lucky one, and you should be grateful for receiving the business. It is not the referral source or even the client who should be grateful for having you. Once you cross that line and start believing you are great, you will lose clients, friends, and referral sources very fast.

36. You need to provide your referral source with updates along the way. Do not forget, you make the referring attorney look bad if he or she runs into the referred client and has no idea what is going on. I have also dropped numerous referral sources, as they never let me know what was going on and I looked like a fool when I saw the client.

37. When you're done with the matter, a phone call to the referral source is *mandatory.* All you need to do is say something like, "I just wanted to thank you for referring _____ to me. I spoke to him/her, and I am being retained." Your referral source will appreciate it.

38. A connection is made if someone remembers you, even if it is for a unique reason. For example, I often drink chocolate milk at breakfast . People used to tease me about "being a kid." Now, people always joke with me because they remember I drink it. The point is, sometimes you just have to do it your way.

39. Not only should you appreciate the client, but you should try to remember that sometimes you are not as close with a client as you think. You always need to maintain the delicate relationship. Most of the time, you are right and the bond is strong, but sometimes you are off. Do not take anything for granted.

40. Research all potential clients. I never did this because I wanted to treat everyone the same, but some people expect it. When you do this, you will be better prepared and ultimately better off. Plus, you can check out any shared connections up front. This is very similar to the upfront analysis we discussed in the interview portion. Connections are always better.

41. Being an expensive attorney can be good and bad. Charging too much versus being a great attorney is a delicate line to walk. I generally tell people I am not inexpensive (somehow a double negative seems to ease the pain a little), but I watch the bills, and if there is major overwork due to the other side, the client will not bear the burden, because I will provide a discount.

42. The faster you respond, the quicker you land a client. If I return a call to a potential client before another attorney, chances are I'm getting hired.

43. Stop by clients' offices if you have time, which you should make. Let them know you were just in the area and came by (you should only drop in on close clients). It will go a long way if they know you are busy but took the time to come by to say hello. Plus, if you really do like them, it's a good time to catch up.

44. Read the paper and remember to follow up. Always look for any information that affects your clients and use it to trigger communication.

45. Say hello in public, when appropriate. I went to breakfast the other day and a client walked in with a friend—they did not see me. On my way out, I went over to say hello. The client said, "I was just thinking about you. Do you know . . . ?" This *always* happens; people always have legal issues. That is the one person who will send you an e-mail two days later and say, "Glad I ran into you. Do you know . . . ?

46. Never leave a place with regret that you did not follow up with someone there. There were many times in my earlier days that I regretted walking out of a place without saying hello to someone. You will truly appreciate it when that person says they have a new matter for you. It's a terrible feeling and the inaction often results in lost money. Don't let their matter be the one that got away.

47. Do favors for clients. Help clients' children. People always know someone who is in or who recently graduated from law school. Speak to them to provide insight on practicing law. Follow up with the client afterward. Good deeds turn into good loyal clients.

48. When you have children, advertise on their uniforms and in their schools. Broaden your exposure. For $300, placing your name on kids' uniforms will allow it to be viewed by thousands of potential clients in the area. Additionally, do not forget to meet the other parents on the team.

49. Constantly remind people what you do. Some people do forget or just do not know. People may not know what a real estate attorney does, or maybe we worked on a particular matter, so someone does not think outside of me outside that area of expertise. Remind them. As I mentioned previously, it's important to try to mention the other areas your firm handles, as well. In fact, I tell people I am a selfish attorney: call me for *everything* and I will find the right people for you, whether it is someone in my firm or not. I want them to call me. If I don't do that type of work, I can at least send them to someone who does. It is not all about making money, it is also about providing a service to the client and helping other people make money. If I have the ability to help, I am the one they call.

50. People want to work with people they like or connect with. Do not be a robot. Your personality is what makes the client want you, not how great your last trial was for somebody else. A free lunch or drinks always helps, as well.

51. Put your cell phone on your e-mails. Clients should be able to reach you on your cell phone. You should be accessible.

52. Spend the extra time on the phone to get to know someone. I was recently talking with a real estate agent and the topic of schools came up. For ten minutes, we talked about our kids and our mutual friends. I was just calling to give an update, but at the end of the conversation, we'd made good connection. I now have a good client, and I had an enjoyable conversation.

Most clients want to talk. I can only say it a thousand times, and I think I have—be thankful for your clients. You are lucky to have them. They are not lucky to have you. Do not *ever* forget this. A friend of mine elected to use me instead of his own personal attorney, and I told him by phone (not e-mail) how much I appreciated him trusting me. You should be thankful for any business you receive.

53. Remind people of events (e.g., concerts, fundraisers). More follow-up. Events are great opportunities to congregate and make introductions. For example, I once told a client about a big event coming up and suggested he attend. He could not have been more thankful for the reminder, plus his bank paid for him to attend. I did not go, but next time I saw him, he remembered, so I was on his mind.

54. Always take the phone call. Few lawyers like to communicate, so the client will be more likely to work with you if you take their calls than an attorney who pushes them aside.

55. Name-dropping is good. I once had a new client interview and I knew three people on the deal. The client felt comfortable because I knew the parties involved. This is the same thing as matter dropping, but it should be limited (e.g., "I have done this type of litigation before"). Remember: do not spend thirty minutes talking about yourself. The meeting is primarily about the client.

56. Sometimes giving a client a discount on a bill helps, as it shows you empathize with them, and it will help you *keep* the client. When you buy something on sale, you feel good. You can make your client feel just as good. (A few hundred dollars here and there can go a long way.)

57. Follow up on the referral sources that ignore you. I saw someone the other day who ignored me for years and suggested we get together. Coincidentally, the next night he called for a drink. (This was even better than me pounding him at a lunch table asking him to send me business.)

58. If someone lets you down, do not alienate them; instead, use it to your advantage. I had a friend who elected to go with a competitor. I stewed about it for months and then ran into him. I told him I wished he would have given me a shot because there is nothing better than representing a friend. Leaving the door open rather than closing it provides more opportunity for business.

A few months ago, I went to lunch and received an e-mail *twenty-seven minutes* after the time we were scheduled to start telling me the other person could not make it (I was talking to a few friends, so it was not a total loss). This guy waited until *twenty-seven* minutes after our meeting time to tell me he was tied up. Inconsiderate ass. How do you respond? You might be tempted to say, "Fuck you. Don't bother ever calling me again." But you must always walk on eggshells and maintain a positive relationship, at least on the surface. If anything, do not burn the bridge because, like you, that person knows ten thousand people, and his story about the missed lunch will not be the same as yours. Sometimes biting your tongue is best, as your paths will inevitably cross again (although it never feels as good as venting).

59. Make sure your spouse knows how to market and network for you. For example, if you're a parent, all those children's parties that your spouse attends provide a lot of new contacts and people who might not be in your normal sphere, so having a spouse who knows how to network for you, is always a good thing. I have three kids and I am now part of the circuit, but my point is that if you are meeting good new people, there's no reason they should not know what you do for a living. Plus, if I am going to miss a football game to attend a children's party, I can at least get a new client out of it.

60. When it comes to corporate clients, stay close and in touch with as many people as you can at the company. If your *only* contact leaves the company, you are done.

61. Stay calm in a dispute with a client. I have a client who felt insulted (for the wrong reason) and suggested our attorney-client relationship was over. Rather than offend him (or even worse, tell him to go fuck himself after he wrote me a scathing e-mail), I sent him a note telling him it was never my intention to affect him in such a negative manner. We spoke about the misunderstanding, and I fortunately (or unfortunately) am back on the list. Like I said above, do not burn the bridge.

62. Introduce everyone to everyone. The more people you introduce, the more likely you will get referred.

63. Know your "referral business." I had a client suggest that I was not loyal to him because I represented so many people in his profession. I reminded him of my referrals and what I do, and I have introduced him to other people who have similar businesses. I have also saved several of his deals because I give free advice. Some people have a short memory—they just need to be reminded.

64. Always be the first to follow up and thank somebody. Coincidentally, I played golf with a client who set up the golf game with a new referral source. I sent a thank-you note to him first thing the next morning. Sometimes I even have my assistant type the note while I am driving so it arrives faster.

65. Check your e-mails. I know a few attorneys who never confirm lunch. I do not need the aggravation of having to follow up with them. I will find another referral source who responds better. Imagine how they treat their clients.

66. Always market yourself or someone else. It is not all about you. Everyone will be grateful.

67. Carry your Dictaphone with you or have easy access to it. You always need to remind yourself to follow up about something. If you forget and miss three opportunities, you just went from a nice car to a moped because of that lost income.

68. Try to put off the last part of billing until the main events go down. For example, when I am at the end of negotiations, I wait until the lease is signed before sending the final bill. If the client sees the actual result, they are more apt to pay, and they will be happier in the end because they can see what you did. If they are happy, they will come back.

69. When going out anywhere, always check out the room. Never check it out when talking to someone, though. Some real estate agents and other so-called networkers in this area are known for looking over people's shoulders during a conversation to see if someone better is in the room. When the time is right, you need to check out who is there, because saying hello can lead to business. Every opportunity must be acted upon. Do not have regrets for failing to follow up.

70. Be polite to people in the service industry. They also have great referrals. I have made a point of getting to know waiters and valets. They may not look like "big fish," but they have their own personal databases. Plus, they are usually truly nice, genuine, and loyal people.

If you play golf at a club, the staff is a great referral source. Let them know what you do, and do not just ignore them. Helping them also feels better as they are often sincerely appreciative.

71. Referrals to other people are just as important as referrals to yourself. It all leads to more relationships and more business.

72. Try to keep in touch with some of your fellow law school students, even the ones you were not close with. It is an easy referral both ways. Recently, alums from my law school and I have been scheduling lunch for twenty or so people in the area to catch up every four months.

73. Get upset when you lose a client. Whenever a client chooses someone over me, I ask why. Do not be angry or rude—do it professionally. You can always learn how to do it better. The worst part is when you take a client for granted. If you do, you will lose clients more often.

74. Ask clients for business, ask what they are up to, and remind them constantly what *you can do for them*. Don't be afraid.

75. If you encounter any attorney you deal with who annoys you, spend a minute with them anyway. Talk to them. Perhaps you may like them in the end, which is great. If not, at least you have taken a step so that next time you deal with them, they will remember you being nice, and that can make your life easier.

76. Ask clients for introductions. Don't be afraid to ask, "Would you mind introducing me to your friend? I would love to represent them."

77. If you do not get a client, always try to throw out some free advice to make them reconsider their decision. You might say, "I hope your attorney understands this aspect of your case because it is my specialty and it will come up." If you go down, go down swinging. (Do it softly, though. Do not sound upset.)

78. Getting business starts by giving something, whether advice, direction, or, even better, business. If you create income for someone else, most likely he or she will try to reciprocate.

79. Don't neglect referral sources. I just settled a case with an attorney in the same area, a sole practitioner. I then spent some time with him after we were finished. Guess what? He is a referral source because *he has conflicts*. He also asked me if I knew a special type of attorney, as he had a new matter. I gave him a friend's name and immediately shot the friend an e-mail letting him know to expect the call. Not only did I find a referral source for myself, but I found a referral source to send business, and I referred business to another referral source (and friend) who will hopefully now benefit and reciprocate. Two weeks ago, I did not even know this attorney. Conflicts help—everyone can be a source of business or help for you, and you can be the same for them.

80. Politics suck, but it's never bad if you can meet a few politicians. Just say hello and tell them who you are. It's no big deal if they do not remember. The key is that next time you can remind them of when and where you met. I also introduce them to other people at events when I see them. It is good for people to see us together. Good recognition is good for business. Maybe I can get business from them, as well.

81. Do free research for clients at times throughout the year. You need to stay on their minds. From time to time, I am given an updated case that may be relevant to a past client. If this happens to you, send it to the prior client, although nothing is pending. Always be on their minds.

82. Always take the time to reach out, even if you have to go out of your way. Be nice and try to help. It is not always about you.

Many years ago, I knew an attorney who was out of work due to a disability. I felt terrible for him. I called to see if I could help with anything. Nowadays, we maintain a close relationship, and he sends me his conflicts and vice versa. This has all been a result of just being nice.

I once heard that a law firm went under and called a friend who worked for the firm. I told him to call me for anything. He used me as a reference with some of the firms where he applied, which he'd done at my suggestion. Now, I receive *all* of his referrals. Just for *being nice.*

Business will follow if you hold yourself to some basic principles—help people, *be nice,* and think about others before yourself.

83. When you meet people, find out how they are getting business. Get new information on how to improve your leads (if this book has not addressed that entirely).

84. Do not forget how to practice law. And be sure to incorporate the advice from earlier.

A. Better communication makes clients happier to refer to you. You want them to say, "My attorney always calls me back."

B. Being positive not only makes you a better person to be around, but also one who receives referral business. This makes you a better lawyer.

C. Caring about your clients and taking their matters personally will only develop your *passion* to help them. Clients will recognize the passion because that is what they want. I have never heard a client say they wanted to hire an attorney without passion. Build that reputation. The passionate attorney gets the referrals.

85. Do everything you can to help. I once went to an event and was talking about summer camps with a guy I just met. I took his card and wrote down the names of a few summer camps. On the following Monday, I sent him an e-mail with the information on my son's camp. It only took me five minutes, but now he will remember me as the lawyer who went out of his way. People send business to good people.

86. Always ask the client how they were referred to you. First, you need to thank the source. It can also remind you of the other sources that are out there.

87. Have your computer networked with your cell phone. You would be surprised how much easier it is to read and respond to e-mails over the weekend while watching football when you can use your cell phone. Plus, your response time is faster.

88. Go the extra mile. Have you heard that a friend's son got engaged? Reach out to him. Always do what you would want for yourself if the situation were reversed.

89. Use social media wisely.

A. During college football season, post about your team and take some jabs at others. First, it is fun—very fun. Second, it gets mini "computer conversations" going with a number of people. Now you are reconnected. (It just so happens that college football gets people excited more than any other sport, but this approach can apply to all sports.)

B. Weekly events like concerts are good for posts, as everyone has an opinion (and it's good for follow-up). Pictures are good, too, especially of your kids. Connect with as many people as you can. Remember, everyone knows ten thousand people.

C. See who everybody knows. Do you have an appointment with someone? Check out their social media page, friends, and connections. If you have a mutual friend or relationship, try to bring that person up in conversation. Now you have a connection with that person.

D. Read the social media sites every day to see what is happening with everyone and follow up in certain situations. For example, "I saw you went to _____. We ate there also months ago." The more you send out, the more people will remember you, and you will be on their minds.

E. Nobody wants to hear about your thousand vacations. All it does is rub your good life in their faces.

F. Stay away from anything political. Once you offend people, you lose business.

G. Do not post any compromising pictures. They never go away. Many employers and prospective clients will view your social media sites and could make a decision regarding your character based on them.

90. When you have a moment, call a client or referral source and ask what they are up to. Go out with them. Try to connect some more. When you communicate, you are on their mind. About 30 percent of the time, a client will ask you a brief question and about 10 percent of the time, the client will have a new matter for you. Always interact at meals or happy hours.

91. You will get more clients if you dress well and look put together than if you look shabby. (Also see #94)

92. You should always be on the phone while driving if allowed by law. (No dialing, though! Pull over.)

93. If you are an attorney who calls someone at 7:30 a.m. or 9:30 p.m., or on the weekend, you are showing that you are an attorney who cares. This goes a long way in the relationship.

94. Like the cover of this book, you need to try and dress for the potential client. Some clients do not want the formal stiff attorney look with the suit and tile. Try to anticipate, but when in doubt, more formal is best.

SUMMARY

Now you are ready to generate business. You understand the nature of bringing in the business, how to find it, and how to create it. It's not very hard. Try to be good to others. In essence, *give, give, give*. You need to remind yourself to follow the basic tips, ideas, and concepts outlined here. If you do, you will develop a database, a referral network, and business for yourself.

A FEW BASIC TIPS TO AVOID JAIL

I believe that 50 percent of all lawyers have accidentally broken one of the two following rules in their first three years of practicing:

1. If a person files bankruptcy, you cannot continue pursuing your claims against them without court approval. Try not to break this rule, as you will lose your license and may end up in jail.

2. You cannot threaten someone with a license revocation, crime, etc. if they do not settle or pay your client. This is called extortion. I probably receive three letters *a year* from new, aggressive attorneys extorting my clients. Usually, I call their principal and suggest they retract. The point is, do not be that associate. Again, try not to break this rule, as you will lose your license and may end up in jail.

SUMMARY

Number one is easy to avoid because now you know the rule.

Number two – as a reminder, do not make or send a stupid comment or e-mail or letter to someone extorting them, hoping to gain an edge for your client.

CLOSING STATEMENT

There you have it: how to get started, how to practice, how to generate business, and even two tips on how to keep your license. Nothing in this book has ever been taught to us in law school.

Do not just *read* this book. Practice it, and apply the information. Reread it often.

Everything is what you make of it. Simply going to lunch does not get you business. You must listen and follow the guidelines herein—and always follow up. Many of the most well-known attorneys in town have come to me to ask why I have so much business or why I get more out of functions than they do. My answer? Simply by trying, and trying, and trying. I never stop, because nothing is a one-and-done. Apply all that you can. You will enjoy your practice, your life, and your clients more than ever. You will appreciate the attorney-client relationships you have. You will not be a self-centered, arrogant, elitist know-it-all. You will be the new brand of attorney.

Good luck on your journey.

ABOUT THE AUTHOR

Greg R. Cohen (Partner) born Pittsburgh, Pennsylvania, September 12, 1971, admitted to The Florida Bar, 1996. Education: University of Miami (B.A., 1993); University of Miami School of Law (J.D., 1996). Practice Areas: Residential and commercial real estate and loan transactions, including a focus on sales and loan transactions, issuance of title insurance, business transactions and development transactions. Furthermore, clients consist of sellers and purchasers of residential and commercial real estate (land, retail, office) and businesses, institutional lenders on commercial and residential loan transactions, real estate agents, title insurance underwriters regarding transactional work and claims work, builders, developers, and landlords and tenants regarding residential and commercial lease transactions. He has lectured to various professionals involved in real estate, including surveyors, title insurance agents, real estate agents, paralegal groups and other lawyers (for approved Florida Bar CLE credits). Mr. Cohen formerly served as the Chairman of the Real Estate Committee of the Palm Beach County Bar Association. He is Board Certified in Real Estate by the Florida Bar. He has also authored *DEAR REAL ESTATE AGENT, THERE ARE ANSWERS*. Mr. Cohen has lectured to attorneys on how to improve their practice, improve their representation of clients, improve their enjoyment of the practice of law, and how to generate a book of business.

51511901R00087

Made in the USA
Columbia, SC
18 February 2019